T0196478

KNOW YOUR ONION

Turning Desires into Realities

Mick Smith

BALBOA.
PRESS

A DIVISION OF HAY HOUSE

Balboa Press books may be ordered through booksellers or by contacting:

Balboa Press
A Division of Hay House
1663 Liberty Drive
Bloomington, IN 47403
www.balboapress.com.au
1 (877) 407-4847

Print information available on the last page.

ISBN: 978-1-5043-1318-6 (sc)
ISBN: 978-1-5043-1319-3 (e)

Balboa Press rev. date: 05/21/2018

The book to read is not the one that thinks for you but the one which makes you think.
—Harper Lee

Table of Contents

Dedication

This book is dedicated to the two most important figures in my life. My wife, Kath, has never doubted that I could convert academic theory and practice into a useable format for anyone who is stuck in a less-than-desirable existence. And my amazing late father, Frank, who passed on at one hundred years of age after encouraging me to do whatever I wanted and not to allow anyone's opinion prevent me from doing anything. He was never judgmental and always encouraging. His favourite quote has stuck with me all these years: "Son, aim high, and you're bound to hit something."

Acknowledgments

It would be an understatement to say that this book would never have materialised had it not been for a lifetime of practicing what I have recorded in the following pages.

Challenge comes from necessity, and I am grateful that my lecturers, students, and clients have all played a part in helping me put pen to paper and finally getting this book to print by challenging me at every step.

Anyone who has completed research under the watchful and critical eye of a thesis mentor knows the frustration of criticism; it is the encouragement that comes from this criticism that motivates you. My studies in psychology and motivational interviewing heavily influence this book.

Students who are hungry for knowledge keep you alert and help you question what you teach; there are too many eager students who have tested me over the years to mention, but I certainly thank them all.

To my clients who provided the inspiration for me to help others by writing this book, I am humbled that you trusted me with your innermost secrets and desires and allowed me to refine the interactions we have had and personalise them to assist you in your endeavours.

Introduction

In the movie *City Slickers,* there is a scene where Jack Palance's character, Curly Washburn, is explaining the one and only meaningful thing in life to Mitch Robbins (played by Billy Crystal). Mitch is a disillusioned man experiencing the Wild West as a present to help him overcome his depression and anxiety over his significant birthday.

Curly tells Mitch there is only one thing in life that matters, and Mitch is excited to hear what that one thing is.

The key focus in the scene is Curly's gloved one finger that he holds up for Mitch to look at. Curly doesn't give any specific meaning of this finger, to Mitch's frustration; he merely explains that the one thing that is symbolised by his finger is different and unique to everyone.

Like Curly's explanation, many self-improvement/motivation books focus on the one thing but fail to show you what that one thing is or indeed how to find it, personalise it, and recognise it for yourself. Advice is offered on what to do *when* you identify it, but in reality, the one thing you are all looking for and what you need help with first still remains a frustrating mystery.

In the following chapters, I will help you identify not only your one thing (your finger or however you choose to personalise your goal) but also strategies and behaviours to turn it from a hypothetical consideration into a tangible reality.

Knowing Your Onion will help you identify your goal, your finger.

The tools explained in **DARNitCAT** in later chapters will show you why you are where you are, how you got there, and why you will stay there unless you follow the simple things identified in this book, starting right now.

DARNitCAT is an acronym used in Motivational Interviewing to identify the individual areas of reflection and reasoning that guide you to your ideal goal and why you feel it is important to you.

DARN represents your: Desire; Ability; Reason and Need to achieve your goals. Once this is established CAT represents your Commitment; Action and Taking steps to implement the changes that you will need to make in your life to achieve the goal (s).

DARN is outlined in detail in chapter 5. Chapter 6 covers the elements of CAT in detail.

If you begin to apply the tools described here and question the things you have always done (and still do), you can change and improve every element of your life.

Many self-help publications outline generic motivational ideas to get you going. However, motivation is a state, not a trait, and unless you see yourself totally and wholly in the situations you have identified for yourself, then that motivation is not merely liable to wane; it most definitely will.

DARNitCAT identifies you and your unique motivators, not everyone else's or generic descriptions of motivation. It is specific to you alone and what makes you unique. The chapters and their content are easily identifiable to you, and the process simple to follow. Be warned, however: while it is simple, it's not easy. Anything worthwhile takes time and effort, so be prepared.

This book will show you how to get into a pattern of sustainable rewarding change in your life, following methods used by the best health and wellness professionals.

You are the most knowledgeable and appropriate person to assist you. No one knows you as well as you do, so why wouldn't you take charge of your life? Mentors and motivators should be facilitators assisting you to construct, obtain, and achieve your goals. Their role should not be to formulate goals for you.

This explanation is simple, and although it is easy to say it's simple, the old adage goes: "When you're up to your ass in alligators, it's hard to remember the initial objective was to drain the swamp." This suggests good ideas with good intentions may be slightly more problematic when you try to act on them.

We are all a unique product of a combination of genetic and environmental conditions. In order to ensure you are getting the best support you need to identify what it is you want and how to get it, you need to dig deep and identify your motivation.

It is hard for most people to see themselves as different from what they are now, primarily because they have never experienced anything different and find it difficult to imagine.

Thinking differently requires imagination; psychologists call this creative visualisation. Imagination is empowering, particularly when it is driven by motivation, and the strongest motivators of all are those that are intrinsic to you.

As an example, you may desire wealth and prosperity. Unfortunately, those desires are without substance, intangible, without specifics attached to them. Is it really money you want? After all, it's only paper or numbers on a bank statement.

Money may be what you need to satisfy what it is you measure wealth and prosperity by and provide the means to obtain what you really want.

If you can't envision what money will do for you to satisfy your intrinsic motivators, you will never have enough money to do anything more than you are already doing.

The process of adaptation is often slow and even insidious at times. You can wind up at a stage in life questioning, "How did this happen? How did I get like this?"

Unfortunately, without conscious effort, your destiny can be somewhat predictable, and when you analyse these questions honestly, the answers are fairly obvious.

If you smoke, drink, and don't exercise, chances are you won't have a healthy physique, so there is a consequence to your behaviour; if you want a different consequence, you merely change the behaviour.

But what can you do to make the necessary changes to ensure things don't carry on like this (or go from bad to worse)? How do you get motivated to engage in a process of change?

By identifying and following the information here you can alter, change, or delete the behaviours that have become habitual and left you on your present course.

This book assists you in identifying your motivators, lets you set specific goals, helps you target behaviour that will ensure you achieve those goals, and provides strategies to ensure you stay on track.

Most importantly, identifying your deepest intrinsic motivators helps you turn this knowledge into meaningful, workable, and rewarding practice to bring about positive change in your life.

How to Use This Book

This book is about motivation. The purpose of the book is to help you identify yours. It describes the different types of motivation that directly influence you; You must understand your most intrinsic motivators, the things that make you feel good about yourself, what you do and why you do it (or not).

Motivation grows from three key ingredients: inspiration, contemplation, and dedication. Inspiration is your idea, your dream, your desire for something; health, wealth, and happiness cover most bases in this regard.

Inspiration is the vision that you can achieve something, contemplation is how deeply you have considered the effort required to achieve the vision and whether the sacrifices required are worth the effort, and dedication is to what extent you are prepared to make the changes and sacrifices necessary to turn a vision into reality.

This book looks at the way you view your understanding of the world and your place in it. If you are actively attempting to achieve goals or plan changes in your life, then the tasks set out within later chapters allow you to investigate your behaviour changes and determine where you need to make them to achieve your goals.

Before making changes or developing goals, you must understand what drives your motivation to change. This book also discusses the different types of motivation and how they affect your actions and behaviour.

When reading any material written about motivation, it is important to ensure that you can identify yourself in the information presented. It is very easy for authors to present their perspectives of motivation and offer a self-disclosure of what motivates them. I have carefully presented the information in this book in a generic sense and avoided the trap of promoting my own enthusiasm, motivators, and goals. The purpose of these exercises is to ensure that you formulate, consolidate, and participate in affirming goals, behavioural changes, and desires that you identify with and wish to pursue.

The book covers distinct areas for your understanding and consideration. These are progressive programmes, with examples and explanations to assist you in using the tools identified in each chapter. Take the time to practice the various programmes identified. Work through each one and return when ideas become more consolidated and as you come to understand the importance of how various aspects affect the design of goal achievement. Remember that each phase of setting goals may be altered many times, changed completely, or merely tweaked. Nothing in the world of motivation and goal setting need be observed as a life sentence. Think of each progressive step as a refinement and a lesson learnt.

This book also explores motivating factors that impact on your life, either negatively or positively; are you currently driven by extrinsic or intrinsic motivators, or have you become amotivated? If you have clear and direct desires and goals, this book will help you focus on the progressive steps towards attainment and success. If you're still unclear what it is you really want but are determined that life can be better, then this book will help you define what that is and what it looks like.

Regardless of what stage you are at, working through the tasks in later chapters of this book will define what you have, what you lack, and what you need to succeed. Knowing your strengths is easy; admitting your weaknesses takes some effort, but ultimately, identifying both is the most important thing you need to do to move forward.

What ability you have may surprise you; what is taught here is how to recognise those abilities and overcome weaknesses. You will strengthen and enhance your abilities once you identify what motivates you.

Completing the tasks within the chapters helps you to identify what your motivators are, those that move you forward or hold you back from achieving your goals in all aspects of your life.

It is intentional that there are two ways to approach this book.

Firstly, merely read it.

Getting to grips with the terminology used in *Know Your Onion* helps. As you read this book, you identify the real you: your situation, your needs, your future, and how your past has an influence on where you are right now. Working through the chapters will identify what it is you really want from life and how to get it. You will gain knowledge about relationships and how your interactions with others can promote your goals and desires, help define your objectives, and put realistic time frames in place.

Many well-intentioned resolutions related to making changes in your life are doomed to failure because the expectations are unrealistic. Not enough planning has been done. This book helps you determine the priorities you need to establish to set realistic and achievable goals. Life changes are a step-by-step process; sometimes, however, this involves a backward step or two, and this book helps you get over obstacles and the inevitable disappointment along the way.

Secondly, engage with it. The insights and tasks identified in the book enable you to study the concepts or actively engage in them.

This book can be regarded as a textbook that you constantly refer to once you have established that you really do want to change something in your life. Refer to the book each time you prepare to attack a new goal or behavioural change; simply follow the processes in the following chapters to make sure you have the desire, ability, reason, and need to turn dreams into reality.

This Book

Chapter 1.

The first chapter describes how you can get to know your onion.

Unless you fully understand yourself, including your past successes and failures, likes and dislikes, it is unlikely you will get very far in understanding how you can move towards behavioural changes that are likely to assist you in realising goals and desires.

Knowing your own onion is a critical look at what keeps you where you are and why, and what you need to focus on to change things.

How schemas are developed is discussed, along with an explanation of how your thought processes work and how they have made you who you are and why you think like you do.

The different types of motivation that influence you are outlined and explained in depth.

The basics of wants and needs are identified through Maslow's theory and how you can define your own personal needs and turn them into concrete goals.

The following chapters direct you step by step to adapting to changes.

Chapter 2.

This chapter describes and analyses the four primordial drivers. As you read and understand the parameters around these drivers, you need to be brutally honest with yourself. You are encouraged to write some of the things you identify with under each of these drivers.

This chapter looks at exactly what defines you. To understand behaviour change, you must first understand your current behaviour fixation: what you do and why you do it.

Identifying your four subliminal drivers will help you take a critical look at your behaviour. In this area, we investigate the primordial concepts of these drivers: fear, expectation, necessity, and habit.

Chapter 3.

Failure is a fact of life, and minor failures are the reason you may have given up on attempting change for yourself in the past. Einstein said, "I have not failed. I have merely attempted ten thousand things that didn't work."

This chapter outlines the four Rs of failure. Recognising these four approaches to goals explains why they have led to failure in the past.

Recognising your own past failures by identifying with these explanations helps you review what went wrong and why. Looking at past failure and analysing your approaches helps you understand what real motivation looks like.

Past failure is likely to have been because of reluctance, rebellion, rationalising, or resignation.

Chapter 4.

This chapter ensures that your goals and desires are focussed on the exact vision you have of yourself in your new environment.

This chapter explores the importance and confidence that you have to complete the tasks necessary for you to achieve the goals you set.

Your reasoning under these two concepts is also questioned.

This area helps to explain why you consider the level of importance and confidence you have and how to increase them, if required.

This chapter establishes a stronger understanding of what these two concepts mean. Importance and confidence establish the foundation for the behavioural changes you will need to make to realise your goals and desires.

The concepts described here are derived from motivational interviewing techniques. The concepts outlined in self-determination theory are also discussed.

Chapter 5.

This chapter outlines the real toolbox you need to work with towards achieving your goals and desires. Like importance and confidence, these tools assist in strengthening the reasons why you put yourself through a process of change. Return to these concepts throughout your change process.

DARNitCAT is another motivational interviewing concept, incorporating theories such as rational emotive behaviour and client-centred learning. It explores your desires, abilities, reasons, and needs for setting goals in your life around tangible parameters and what those goals actually look like. It emphasises the need to initiate today to begin immediately implementing some forward momentum towards your goals.

Chapter 6.

At this point, you have merely read a book (maybe just another book). Without action, the reading itself is at best just increasing your understanding of motivation (at worst, it adds confusion about what your desire is).

This final concept in this programme is establishing your commitment to the task, the actions you plan to take, and taking the steps to initiate those actions.

What is commitment? What does it take to say you are committed to something? Is your desire matched by your commitment? How is action achieved? What is the appropriate level of action required? Even if commitment and action is high, this means nothing if you do not take steps and actually do something to make the changes necessary to achieve goals and realise your desires.

1

Understanding Your Onion, Schemas, Motivation, and Maslow

The true sign of intelligence is not knowledge but imagination.
—Albert Einstein

The tough part about making any change in your life is firstly understanding yourself. Development is a drawn-out process, and a lot of what has made you what you are has gone unnoticed. Much of what has formed the person you are to date has been via subliminal messaging, repetitive and reinforced behavioural expectations, and family, environmental, cultural, educational, and vocational experiences.

Perceptions, memories, encounters, and actions collect in your subconscious. They can be tightly bound in formed schema that can be defined as your onion. They are divided into either positive or negative experiences.

The onion analogy is appropriate in that if you have ever peeled one, you know that it can make you cry and consists of many tightly packed layers.

An onion is a very dense and hard object; it's also difficult to peel and to separate those layers. Peeling it also produces a physiological reaction (crying). This can take a bit of effort; however, once you've done it and take a closer look each layer, it is really soft and pliable, and there is less crying.

Like an onion, you compact your negative and positive experiences into one big mass. Within those layers lie your desires mixed with your abilities, needs, and reasons, as well as all the negative perceptions that are holding you back from making the behavioural changes required to change.

As you attempt to recognise what your desires are, you will be challenged many times. Where your abilities might come from and the difficulties you may encounter in making changes to the habitual routines that keep you from moving forward will be questioned constantly. What influences habits is often indecipherable and difficult to visualise; however, the level of success you achieve is directly proportional to your motivation.

You identify with a total compilation of life experiences rather than identifying the layers (individual experiences and responses) separately. Knowing what made them positive or negative is significant.

By confronting and reviewing each layer (success or failure), you reduce or increase the overall significance that the experience has had on you as either positive or negative.

If a combined set of experiences has resulted in either a positive or negative memory, reviewing the experience and dismissing or reinforcing various issues may give you a better understanding of how approaching things differently had a significant effect on the outcome. The result may be the same, but at least you know what to do (or not to do) next time to achieve a more favourable outcome rather than to totally avoid the situation in which the experience was created.

Knowing your personal onion is very important in reducing stress and negativity. Confronting the barriers presented by your onion is imperative to allow you to move forward and make positive changes in your life.

Making a personal onion involves identifying those things that are difficult for you to deal with. Looking at your fear (chapter 2), you can target each layer of your onion and see how each has a domino effect on the others. By identifying fears through this process, you can look at whether the tools you have identified in your ability list (chapter 5) are sufficient to deal with your fear as a whole or as a specific layer.

If you find you have insufficient tools accessible to you, the task is to then define what else you require to tackle a specific layer of your onion and identify how to obtain those tools.

The purpose of exposing the layers of your onion is to identify the negative actions and responses that you have maintained through habit (chapter 2) that prevent you from moving forward.

Once identified and analysed, you can describe the changes needed to turn negative reinforced habits into positive habits. Positive changes are reinforced through your desires, reasons, and needs that you attach to your desired goals.

Remember that your current perceptions and actions are a result of your personal experiences, upbringing, educational and social pursuits, genetics, and environmental constraints. These have all contributed to the development of your own collection of schema. Schemas drive your habits, which in turn are the foundation blocks for your fears, expectations, and needs. Your goal is to change your habits.

What Are Schemas?

Schemas are patterns of thoughts or behaviours. They are collections of your experiences—throughout your life—that are organised into categories of information. Planted in your subconscious, they provide a mental structure. They are responsible for connections, understanding, and responding to situations and relationships from information constructed from preconceived ideas.

As a result, your actions and behaviours are limited by the depth and extent of the schema you have been exposed to and that have subsequently become imbedded into your subconscious.

Your development of schema is influenced by familial, vocational, educational, environmental, spiritual, and cultural factors. Schemas are the reason you see the world and everything in it as you do; they influence your likes and dislikes. Your attention is directed to things you are attracted to and have knowledge of by schema.

However, when you are confronted with conflicting information or totally new concepts, you need to re-evaluate the new information, interpret the contradictions, and either distort them to fit into existing schema or develop new ones. This can be a smooth transition, as the subconscious can handle some developments with relative ease, depending on how entrenched the belief is.

Schemas are relatively robust and tend to remain unchanged, even when presented with contradictory information. Instead, you tend to develop additional schema to influence behaviour in a more defined situation. In other words, you develop a more discerning view of complex or contradictory information.

When you embark on a journey of behavioural change, you need to challenge some existing schema you have developed and are responsible for the well-rehearsed behaviours that you currently action.

In your most primordial sense, you behave due to four subconscious drivers:

- fear
- expectation
- necessity
- habit

It is important to recognise what these drivers are and how to recognise the individual elements under each of them.

Motivation Is an Inside Job

> Once something is a passion, the motivation is there.
> —Michael Schumacher

What exactly is motivation?

Motivation is the fuel that actions your four primary drivers. Motivation is a necessary component for change and is important in all aspects of your life.

Without motivation, there would be no life. You are motivated to eat, breathe, drink, sleep, protect yourself, and seek comfort. Each of these variables is unique to you, but what drives these motivators is not static. Motivation can change according to the situation and your needs. Repeated throughout this book, we reinforce that motivation is a state, not a trait. What motivation looks like and how strong a driver it is, is dependent on what you really want and how badly you want it.

Studying the three basic forms of motivation outlined below will assist you to question where your motivation for a particular action or habit is coming from and why. Regular questioning of actions and habits helps prevent disappointment and mundane routine, which in turn robs you of your most valuable item: your time.

Motivation is recognised in three basic forms:

1. **Intrinsic**
   When you are intrinsically motivated, you engage freely. Intrinsic motivation refers to motivation that comes from *inside* an individual.

   The desire to engage in an activity or task is as important as the goal. It is a source of challenge and enjoyment; therefore, it is the motivating factor regardless of any reward received for achieving a result.

   Intrinsic motivation is sustained by the belief that you can control events and outcomes.

   If the focus of the goal is solely on the end rewards, such as money, grades, or an engagement, motivation may be described as extrinsic. As an example, if the desire and focus of the intrinsic motivation is to win an Olympic medal, you will recognise that the steps to achieve that desire may include some decidedly extrinsic motivators.

   Should the goal not be met, the engagement process—say the training required to win—may wane, and motivation may be lost.

2. **Extrinsic**

Why is it lost? Because it isn't interesting enough anymore, as the expectations have not been met.

The motivation to engage may be prompted by significant others or events in your life rather than specifically for you. This is the essential difference between intrinsic and extrinsic motivation: how much is for you, and how much is influenced by others?

The dynamics of any behaviour involve the expectation of a reward for engaging in it. Extrinsic motivation is reliant on contingencies, which are things in the future that are possible but not definite. This refers to motivation that comes from *outside* an individual. The motivating factors are externally prompted by a need, perhaps including rewards like money or grades to ensure a better job, lifestyle, or relationship.

These rewards are expected to provide satisfaction and pleasure, so they could be considered intrinsic; however, the tasks required to achieve them may not.

Consistent achievement of the goal will dictate the duration of acceptance of the less-than-motivating factors necessary to maintain it.

3. **Amotivation**

When you are amotivated, you display a distinct lack of motivation; there is no perception of contingency between the behaviour and the outcome.

There is a serious risk associated with amotivation.

Amotivational syndrome is a psychological condition associated with diminished inspiration to participate in social situations and activities, with episodes of apathy caused by an external event, situation, substance (or lack of), relationship (or lack of), or other cause.

The sense of despair from continually not seeing success in any form and the inability to foresee light at the end of the tunnel can lead to amotivation. Inactivity is an attempt to improve a situation, hoping it will change without effort. This can lead to an increase in symptoms of depression and anxiety.

Where does motivation come from?

External

External factors are influences that affect how you act or perform to obtain a positive end state (result) or avoid a negative end state.

The external factors that influence your motivation are driven by your four subconscious drivers: fear, expectation, necessity, and habit.

How can an external motivator influence your behaviour?

An example is, you go to a job that you don't particularly like, *but* at the end of the week, you get a paycheck that meets your needs, which is a positive end state.

In the same way, you may have external factors where you are motivated to avoid a negative experience or end. By doing the work you are supposed to do at your job and doing it to a satisfactory level, you may avoid getting fired.

Introjected

With introjected motivation, you are taking prompts from the environment and internalising the behaviour.

Motivation that is considered introjected comes from experiences in your everyday life that you may take for granted and act on without reflection. The behaviour is seldom questioned; rather, it is a robotic exercise developed over time.

Examples of introjected motivation are where you are acting out of obligation such as paying your bills on time; obeying traffic laws; and caring for your family.

Identified

Identified motivation is when the reason to engage in an activity is internalised and the performance of the behaviour is considered to be valuable to you. The activity is performed with a sense of choice regulated through identification of the activity and the subsequent benefits to you.

Identified motivators are what you *really* want; the purpose of this book is to assist you in focussing more and more on this type of motivation. The ideal identified motivator is waking every morning and jumping out of bed because you are on your way to a job or an activity that you love.

A big paycheck for the job you do is identified, but it is also considered external if that's the only reason you work at that job.

A big paycheck is an extrinsic motivator for doing a job if, in all other respects, it is less than satisfying and the money does not provide something special for you.

A job that provides stimulus to you and is intrinsically motivating because of what you actually do in your work is more desirable.

Remember, however, motivation is a state, not a trait, and even the most fabulous and rewarding job on earth is likely to throw you a curve ball now and then.

When you identify with your motivators, you can also understand where and why your state of motivation changes.

Situational

In some situations, your motivation may be strong, yet the same motivation may change if the situation itself changes.

Take, for example, an athlete. The motivation to train may be high while the weather is fine and the sun is shining, yet the motivation to do the same regime of training may be reduced if it's blowing a gale, the temperature has dropped, or it's raining cats and dogs, and you have to go on a five-mile run.

The strength of the intrinsic motivation (in the above case, this is the competition factor) will keep the athlete focussed on the training, no matter what the conditions are.

Feelings of Satisfaction

It may seem a no-brainer that motivation is increased because there is a feeling of satisfaction in doing whatever you are engaged in.

However, satisfaction represents myriad specific emotions that are individualised. Satisfaction is also graded from a negative perspective to a positive one.

You are often asked in opinion polls to rate your level of satisfaction with a product ranging across a linear selection, for example, 0–10, where 0 equals not satisfied at all and 10 means totally satisfied. People's opinion and satisfaction are likely to be as varied as the people undertaking the poll. So why do you consider satisfaction here?

The answer to this is because you can accept things that are not completely satisfying. Why? Because they are not altogether negative and give you satisfaction that is sufficient enough for you to accept it as okay.

If something is okay, you seldom seek to improve on it, until is no longer acceptable.

You will habitually accept as satisfactory many things that have the potential to be improved; they could be better for you.

However, if the strength of the motivation to do so is not sufficient to engage in making the necessary changes, you won't do it.

Level of Attainment

How far you get doing something is also an indicator of the motivational level you have for engaging in the behaviour.

Golf is a rather humorous example of this for me. I don't play very often, but my motivation for doing so can be vastly improved by performing one really good shot.

In business and work, attainment may be seen as a promotion or an increase in productivity; in sports, winning or improving on a past performance; in social status, election to office may indicate that you have reached whatever it is you see as recognition for the effort necessary to achieve it.

Behavioural Persistence

Behavioural persistence is where you have reached a level of attainment and gained satisfaction from the *process* as well as the result.

When you are aware of the situational factors that created the environment that contributed to success, you are more likely to continue this practice in other areas and with other projects.

Behavioural persistence ensures that you repeat the success process often until subconsciously, all you act upon or engage in becomes successful, positive, and rewarding.

How long you continue to perform a particular behaviour will be directly proportional to the intrinsic motivation you get from performing it.

Take, for example, many volunteers working long hours to help save whales, operate a soup kitchen for homeless people, or collect door to door for a worthy cause. What drives them? Again, the reasons will be varied, but it's a good bet that the feeling they get for helping others is a strong motivator.

Of course, this can also work the other way. If the level of attainment falls short, or you fail to achieve your goal (or even if progress is slow or unrewarding), motivation wanes, and as a result, you will embed negative subconscious predictions that in any same situation, your level of satisfaction will be low. The behavioural persistence in this instance will be to avoid the situation.

Important

When you are preparing to engage in a behaviour that is intended to help you reach a goal, it is important that you are prepared and as ready as you can be.

Eliminate as many distractions as possible before you start. Set sufficient time aside; always try and end your engagement with your project on a positive note so that you will look forward to your next session.

Don't let perfectionism become an excuse for never getting started.
—Marilu Henner

Who Are You?

You are a product of your genetics and your environment. You are then moulded over time by your culture, teachers, peers, and family; refined by circumstances and beliefs; guided by likes and dislikes, the known and the unknown; and compromised by health, education, laws, and significant others.

Okay, sounds fair enough. But if you take a real hard look at this, the only issue out of your control is the genetic bit.

Most people have heard of Sigmund Freud; he was a psychologist (well, neurologist actually) who developed some controversial concepts about our development; he had some weird ideas, as well, but importantly, he produced some useful tips for understanding why you are what you are.

Freud came up with this idea that we were essentially made up of three parts: the id, the ego, and the super ego. Wikipedia informs us that these three parts of the "psychic apparatus" are interactional; the id is "a set of uncoordinated instinctual trends"; the super ego "is critical and moralizing," while the ego represents organisation: it "mediates between the id and the super ego."

This concept has stuck with other experimenters and researchers who followed him: Jung, Adler, Ericson, Maslow, Rogers, and many others who have tried to promote human development in some form or another.

The commonest denominator between these pioneers was that they basically agreed that as an individual, you are a product of a number of variables, some beyond your control, but the majority are within it.

To give a more reasonable correlation to these parts of your persona (and take a bit of poetic license in the process), the suggestion is that you can understand this concept a bit better by speaking of the child, the adult, and the conscience.

Essentially, this means that throughout your developing years, in a clinically normal childhood, your child was let loose; it played and got into mischief, tried some things, got some success and some failure.

However, all the while, you were guided by the conscious, which grew along with you as your knowledge and experience level increased (usually in the form of your parents and teachers, who gave you insight into right and wrong, good and bad, safe and unsafe).

They instilled laws, rules, and morals that modified your behaviour so that when you grew up, you would be a model citizen, an adult yourself who would in turn instil all of those things into your children, and so it goes on.

So while yes, you are who you are because of all of these things, it doesn't mean you have to stay that way if you don't want to. You have the ability to

- change your environment,
- challenge you culture, teachers, peers, or family (I didn't say it would be easy),
- rethink your beliefs,
- review your likes and dislikes,
- research the unknown and question the known for validity,
- improve your health,
- expand your knowledge,
- help make change around you, and
- influence others.

You've probably already read a few self-help or motivational books. Did you get enthused and motivated? Did you see the light and shout, "Hallelujah"? Did you identify yourself with the points raised in the text, only to find at the end of the book, you circle back to the point you started from, perhaps even more disillusioned and demotivated than when you started?

How many times have you picked it up and reread it?

The fact (and there is only one) is that a bit of effort is required from you to get things to where you are actually moving forward. This book (or any book, for that matter) is not going to do that for you.

There is not a book written that by merely reading it ensures things will happen for you. At some point, you have to get physically and mentally involved. That's like expecting a trim, fit, athletic body simply by purchasing a membership to the local gym.

When I decided to write this book, the one thing I wanted readers to know from the outset was that my offerings were not merely confined to what is written here. It is designed to be interactive, a workbook that allows you to measure your progress and gain guidance along the way. You are reinforced throughout the book that motivation is a state, not a trait, and if you fall off the programme you set for yourself, we are here to help you get back on it.

Okay, you know about the genetic bit, and you will by now have an understanding of how you perceive things by analysing the three components of your personality: your adult, child, and conscience, so let's move on and get to some more interesting stuff.

Okay, so to answer the question as to how I became me:

Societal and environmental conditions, social accessibility, and changing demographics in families and cultural surroundings have rapidly expanded the influences on vulnerable minds. The access to social media provides multidimensional contradictions to much of what you have accepted in the past.

The level of certainty around many imbedded beliefs is being constantly challenged, reviewed, accepted, discarded, or modified.

Take, for example, young people moving from India to a Western culture. The tradition of arranged marriages presents conflict for many young Indians. They may face challenges and confrontation with the cultural expectations of their parents and elders over the process and its significance in the context of their new environment and culture.

The wearing of traditional dress, such as the burka, has raised outrage and sparked intense emotions in many countries; the backlash on migrants has caused concern and a fight-or-flight response in order to protect their beliefs or abandon them for a new set of cultural rules and expectations.

So true it is for the modern generations, and not just children growing up. You are a part of a period in time that has seen rapid change in technology, and as such, you are able to embrace this new world and move with it or choose to selectively adopt what it has to offer.

How you do this and which way you use these aids is totally dependent on what they can do for you in achieving what it is you want.

Some of the happiest people I know across all ages are those who have made a conscious decision to avoid this rapid technological change and have adopted a much less operational and constructed lifestyle.

There is a small but increasing number of individuals leaving urban areas to live off the land and produce their own food, as an example.

This decision can produce a serendipitous effect. Following a passion and realising your true intrinsic motivators to live this kind of lifestyle can lead to small business opportunities.

Whichever path you take must not be viewed as a life sentence. As I have stated and will state many more times in this book, motivation to do something is not a trait; it is a state, and that can change numerous times over the course of a lifetime (or even in the course of a few minutes).

Imagine you are strongly motivated to a strict diet. The weight is coming off, but the food is bland, and you are constantly hungry; you're getting a bit miserable but still focused on the goal of losing weight. Suddenly, there is a knock at the door, and your partner has ordered a home delivery pizza. The smell is alluring; the imagination of the taste is insufferable. You weaken and grab a slice of heaven.

While the remorse may come back to haunt you, the reality is that it may be that losing weight wasn't a strong enough motivator.

In this instance, you must view the motivation to lose weight not as the stronger intrinsic motivation but the lesser extrinsic motivation. Where you fell over was not having stronger intrinsic motivation to get you past the temptation. While you agreed that you wanted to lose weight, the reason for the loss should have been the intrinsically motivated desire of what to expect when the weight was lost.

The desire was strong; the ability was there, but the reason and need were not established (or at least not strong enough).

At this point, you might want to write down some positive experiences you have had where you have overcome temptations to reach a goal: not socialising, as an example, to study for an upcoming exam; things you have been told that have struck a chord with you and remain imbedded in your memory; things you have experienced that have had a profound effect on you; things that have scared you or made you laugh or cry; things that have made you angry; or things that have made you rethink your beliefs.

All of these things produce emotions, some good, some not so good, and some bad. The important thing is that they produced the emotion in the first place.

Emotions either help you move forward or keep you treading water. To know how you became the person you see in the mirror every day, you need to firstly understand your emotions and what produced them. Secondly, you need to be able to control those emotions.

This isn't as easy as it sounds. Emotions that are produced by new concepts and interactions are the most difficult to control. Here's why:

The older you get, the more life experiences you have had (that is not without recognising that a sixteen-year-old due to circumstances may have met with more experiences than someone in their forties); the number, of course, is different for everyone.

Essentially, emotions are an inbuilt protection mechanism, and in order to do their job, they are constantly checking and analysing myriad new information coming into your senses. (Remember our schemas?)

Here's an example of a negative emotion at work and how our schema advise you to react:

You are walking along and see a lizard in front of you; you have never seen a lizard in your life before, but you have seen a snake and were bitten by it. This was a negative experience, which produced a negative emotion. Your memory searches for a reasonably close facsimile of the lizard and comes up with snake. Your immediate emotion towards the lizard is therefore a negative one.

The same goes for a negative experience at, say, a job interview. The more repeatedly you get rejected after an interview, the more likely your expectation at the next interview will be rejection.

Weighing up your positive experiences against your negative ones has a direct relationship to your expectations.

Positive experiences produce positive emotions, which produce positive expectations, and vice versa; if negative experiences exceed positive ones, you are likely to develop a tendency to see every new experience negatively.

Strengthening your motivation does not have to be done totally on your own. Sometimes, discussing goals and aspirations work well, provided your source of assistance is empathic.

Who you trust to discuss your dreams and desires with also has a directly proportional effect on whether you will have positive or negative experience from it.

Most people have at least one mentor in their lives: a parent or grandparent, teacher, neighbour, family friend, boss, or colleague. There may be more than one mentor available, each with their own level of expertise and wealth of experience.

Discussing your goals with some people may work in the opposite direction. At times, people may be confused by what you are trying to achieve or they know somebody who attempted what you're planning (even if it is nothing like what you have in mind), and they will attempt to dissuade you.

Keep in mind that some potential mentors may be negative towards your ideas. Have they asked you a lot of questions and discussed your responses? If not, they may be uninterested in your ideas or unable to help you.

Don't be discouraged by these responses; keep looking until you find the kind of support you need.

A good mentor is someone who puts themselves in your shoes and understands your motivation. They react with empathy and offer advice only after asking your permission and only after researching and digesting as much as they can about your proposal. They should attempt to direct you to knowledgeable sources to assist you in the decision-making process; they will be there when your motivation takes a hit and help you get back on track or modify your approach.

If you search out a professional mentor, make sure that you are comfortable with talking to them and expressing yourself. Try and find someone with personal knowledge and experience in your proposal.

You also want someone you trust, who will be there when they're needed.

If you plan on being a mentor yourself, it's important that if you offer the hand of help, you don't withdraw it when your mentee strikes a stumbling block and needs you most.

Can You Change Things? Of Course You Can

Consider this:

What if we stifled your inner child's behaviour or, alternatively, let the child run amuck? Could it be that this would produce people with little or no morals or social boundaries? Or alternatively produce those with an overbearing and limiting attitude to the world around us, including appreciation of enjoyable activities?

The point is that you need a bit of child in you to remember how to enjoy yourself and what playing can do for your mood. You also need a bit of adult to show you when you've gone a bit too far; your conscience will help you decide if your behaviour is appropriate.

By now, you may question some of the beliefs you have: the way you look at things, the authority by which you came to those beliefs and actions, and how they've been reinforced. Questioning is a good thing.

Abraham Maslow was noted for his many thought-provoking studies and psychological theories.

My most favourite saying of his was "If your only tool is a hammer, then everything begins to resemble a nail," and it is true.

This means you often see things via a limited perspective; limited by what? Well, by your experience, and so you attack it with the only knowledge you have.

For example, a huge number of people are scared of spiders, but how many people do you know who have actually had a bad experience with a spider?

Maslow recognised a series of needs that we as humans require, either physiologically or spiritually.

Your physiological needs are really pretty basic; your spiritual needs and self-worth needs are much more complex and individualised. Maslow described these through various levels, from the very basic requirements for life (which he described as *deficit needs*, those needs that are required to keep you alive: food, water, shelter), through to *being needs,* described as your ultimate goal achievement, where you identify with your personal desires and measures of success.

What Maslow described is really what makes you who you are, but it equally shows you how you can be what you want to be, if you want it badly enough.

It also shows you how willing you are to accept *lesser* needs if the going gets a bit tough.

Describing these increments in needs is essential at this point for you to start putting some parameters around your needs. As you progress, you will identify how closely your motivation agrees with these needs and if you should change focus.

It is important that whatever you put under these needs, you must be able to visualise clearly. That visualisation should become spontaneous.

Your subconscious mind will order your conscious mind into action when you clearly identify your targets and goals. How to do this is set out in later chapters, but for now, it is important to start making things a bit more specific and personalised to you.

The sooner this gets under way, the sooner you will be achieving all the things you really want, everything you are intrinsically motivated to get. Once these things are etched into your subconscious, nothing will prevent them from happening.

At this point, you should start a diary. You can either do this on your computer or simply buy a notebook and start writing things down. It is important to date all your entries so you can monitor your progress. It is also important to visit this several times a day or more.

If you are always trying to be normal, you will never know how amazing you can be!
—Maya Angelou

Maslow's Hierarchy of Needs

Maslow's hierarchy of needs is a blunt reminder that in reality, humans require very little to survive; what you choose to add to your life is up to you. Whether you need these additions is directly proportional to what they could provide for you above your deficit needs.

Deficit needs: These are described as the necessary components to survive; they include the basic fundamentals of life: food, water, safety, and shelter. What do your basics look like? What are they?

(Write them down in your notebook.)

These needs are also **physiological.** If you have never fought for anything before and have been accepting of everything life throws at you, and you suddenly don't have these things, watch how quickly you will fight with all you have to get them. These needs are about basic survival. Ignore them, and you cease to exist.

Safety needs: Your safety needs are just that: what makes you safe; they are more personalised than physiological needs. They include safety to your physical self, your job, your family, and your health.

Belonging needs: Again, this gets more personalised. This group includes your culture, friendships, and intimate relationships.

Esteem needs: You really start to personalise these needs as your own now. At about this point, you may be scratching your head and wondering what it is that fits this category? These needs define what you see as giving you confidence; self-esteem attributes are those traits you respect in others and what you would like to be respected for.

Self-actualisation: Okay, the nitty gritty stuff.

Under this heading of needs, you really zero in on yourself, looking closely and questioning your prejudices and the facts you accept; what is your mission? Do you have the resources and knowledge to get to where you want to be and who you want to be? These are your **Being needs,** and it's time to be very specific about what these look like.

If you can't visualise it, either it isn't as important as you thought it was or you don't want it badly enough (or you're not convinced of its importance).

A lot of the negative thinking about why you haven't achieved things in your being list is because of your past experiences; remember what the mind does? It recognises those previous experiences. If they were all negative, they resulted in negative emotions. Negative emotions produce protection mechanisms that prevent you from trying again.

By now, you are hopefully starting to think about what it is you truly and sincerely want to be or do. You are starting to visualise specific things happening in your life. However, we're going to come back down to earth for a brief period to consider some things that may be keeping you where you are instead of letting you move on ahead. At this point, we want you to be fully focused, perhaps not on specifics but definitely on making you a better you, whatever that may look like.

Many of your current beliefs, positive and negative emotional responses, may be well and truly engrained into your behaviour, memory, and subconscious. There may be some solid resistance to change from within you.

The key to the success of all of this is to develop an unwavering focus on goals, once you have clearly established what they are.

At this point, you may not yet think of these changes as normal. If this is the case, you've probably never reviewed what you desire in life: what would you really like to be, what do you want to own, and what makes you happy? However, that doesn't mean you can't; it just means you haven't looked at all the reasons that have stopped you focusing on a better you, until now.

How believable these desires are is totally dependent on the strength of the intrinsic motivation you have to achieve them. If you already have some clear ideas, that's great; if not, don't despair. The process is the same for everyone, whether you're just venturing into a new beginning of a better you or you're seeking to improve on what you already have.

It is the purpose of this book to assist you to find what those motivators are and strengthen them.

Everything will be okay in the end; if it's not okay, it's not the end.
—John Lennon

Schema, Types of Motivation, and Maslow

There's a bit to take in from this chapter; you are beginning to identify your motivators, where they come from, and why you maintain certain habits. At this point, consider Maslow's explanation of why you do what you do. To make changes that will last, you need to consider the sacrifices and behavioural changes (effort) required. Is it worth it? Is it sustainable? Remember that changes do not need to be a life sentence. Revisiting your needs regularly and making any necessary changes required along life's journey is important to ensure you don't get stuck in a situation that wastes your time and energy for no reward.

2

The Four Subconscious Drivers: Fear, Expectation, Necessity, and Habit

The Four Subconscious Drivers

You may not even be aware of why you do a lot of what you do and how you do it. Schema, as discussed, gives a clinical explanation of how these subconscious drivers are formed, but in order to see how they influence you personally, it is important to look at what makes you do the things you do.

In order to make any significant paradigm shift in your thinking, it's important to look at *how* you think, now. Most of what you do is based on subconscious drivers, which are

- fear,
- expectation,
- necessity, and
- habit.

Each of these drivers is inseparable from the others. Like a chemical equation, any change to any of these four drivers has a directly proportional effect on the others.

This is important to understand because this is where you influence change at its most primordial level. One of the most amazing things about this is that it is self-fulfilling and gives you a glimpse of just how powerful the recognition of your inner strength is when you choose to challenge it with positive reinforcement.

> # You never want to hear that ticking clock and think, *I had all that time and didn't use it.*
> —J. J. Abrams

Fear

Your most primordial motivator is fear.

Fear is the force that provides the strongest motivation. It is important to understand that while fear can protect you at times, without in-depth analysis of why you are fearful in any given situation, that same fear may prevent you from engaging in something rewarding. Identifying what your fears are, why you have them, and how to address them helps you face and conquer them.

Thousands of years ago, fear meant being eaten by a bigger or faster predator, the possibility of low or no food resources, loss of warmth and shelter, and lack of fresh water. You're back at Maslow's needs again.

Over time, what you fear has increased beyond these deficit needs, although for all humankind, they still remain extremely relevant. For someone starving on the plains of Ethiopia, they are of course the most urgent and foremost in their minds. However, for Westerners, fear has become far more complex and multidimensional.

What you fear is heavily influenced by society and cultural expectations, legal demands, financial issues, family and vocational challenges, and a host of other aspects that have influenced the development of your schemas.

It is a worthwhile exercise at this point to write down and record your fears as you consider them now. Put names to these fears and comment on their intensity. (These are notes for you to review later.)

In this context, fear is seen as a *negative reinforcer*. In other words, you do things because you will avoid a negative consequence. For example, "If I don't go to work, I won't get paid, and I won't be able to pay the mortgage, feed the kids, or fix the car. So if I go to work, those things won't happen."

The value of the work in this context becomes less of a motivator than what the reward for working is. In this case, the reward is prevention of all of these negative consequences.

In this example, your work is considered to be an *extrinsic* motivator; that's okay to a point, but it can lead to persistent negative and pervasive thoughts about work, which in turn affects your performance at work and at play.

Fear is everywhere. You are fearful when confronted with a situation you have experienced before; it raises an emotion in you. Fear is also apparent when you are forced to engage in an unknown situation. This is because our schema have recognised a component of that situation that presents to your conscious as potentially dangerous or detrimental to your needs.

Every situation will conjure up a connection with previous experiences. Challenging the initial thought and confronting the fear factor as something real or irrational needs to be a priority. This is an example of reviewing your onion layers. It takes a great deal of effort but ultimately becomes easier once you analyse and review previous thought processes. Releasing yourself from irrational belief and fear is enlightening. If motivation is strong, this task is all the more easily embraced.

Don't let your fear of what could happen make nothing happen.
—Anon.

Fear

Object of Fear	Frequency of Fear	Intensity Related to Family	Intensity Related to Work	Intensity Related to Leisure	Intensity Overall Rating
Serious illness	7	8	9	4	7

In the example above, I have identified a common fear for many people, that of contracting a serious illness. We'll call this person Annie, a forty-two-year-old married working mother of three with a family history of breast cancer.

The frequency of the fear indicates how pervasive this fear is to her. She indicates a high correlation with the illness in part due to historical family experiences compounded by her age, but reinforced by advertising on television and radio urging women to undergo regular breast screening.

Understandably, the intensity of the fear increases when she considers the impact of the disease on her family: "What if I have it? What if it's really aggressive? What happens if it's too late? What will happen to my family? How will it affect them?"

All logical questions.

Considering the impact in relation to work, the intensity is further increased. The fear escalates as the realisation that work and therefore income may be compromised during any period of treatment, rehabilitation, and recovery. This links with the fear already related to family as the decrease in income that may threaten the family's well-being.

Considering the fear in relation to leisure, we see a lessening of fear. There are several ways to explain this lower rating. It could be that due to family and work commitments, there are no real leisure pursuits. Annie may well be so preoccupied with work and family commitments that she has not had time for leisure activities. It may also be considered less of a concern if the leisure activity is less physical or not specific to a fixed agenda, such as reading or listening to music.

The final rating of fear, however, remains high enough to be a pervasive intrusion preventing enjoyment and a happy, fulfilling lifestyle.

How do you interpret these recordings?

There is a strong rationale for the overall fear. Family history explains this. What are the factors that may reduce this level?

If Annie asks herself these questions, it may help reduce the fear to a realistic and manageable level:

- Has a doctor checked me? (mammograms, etc.)
- Does my doctor know my family history? Knowing the history of a patient ensures the practitioner will be more diligent with monitoring and ensure she is reminded of appointments and follow-ups.

- Am I knowledgeable on the current practices and interventions to reduce the risk?
- What testing did my family members have access to?
- How have these things changed since their time?

The rung of a ladder was never meant to rest upon, but only to hold a man's foot long enough to enable him to put the other somewhat higher.

—Thomas Huxley

Expectation

Expectation is another of your fundamental drivers. Knowing the effect of expectation in your life is important to drive behavioural change.

On the plus side, expectation can raise levels of euphoria and excitement. Ideally, you would want all expectation to be a positive experience. Pavlov's experiment with his salivating dogs hearing a bell ring before dinner was served showed how expectation can be triggered by a seemingly minor event that indicated the possibility of a rewarding experience.

Equally, expectation can have a negative response. Imagine the same situation with Pavlov's dogs had the ringing of the bell stimulate a thought response that the dog was about to receive an electric shock.

What is important about expectation is that it should come as a result of preparedness that ensures the best possible outcome. If expectation continually registers a negative response or action, it is clearly time you need to change something.

Expectation, like fear, falls under two distinct categories that are driven by negative or positive reinforcers. To make this a little more complex, you need to consider your specific motivational factors. Are your expectations extrinsically driven or intrinsically driven?

It is very possible that you have no idea what your intrinsic motivators are at this stage. Don't worry; these things will fall into place. It's far better to have them carefully develop into concrete objectives while you work through this book, but it is important to realise the difference between extrinsic and intrinsic motivators and how they affect long- and short-term motivation.

You should consider identifying your motivators and measure the strength around them. This will be explained in later chapters, but it is helpful to consider your perception of them now and then review your understanding as you practice the tasks outlined for you in this book.

Expectation is another driver that becomes embedded in the subconscious. A very basic example, yet a poignant one, is breathing. You don't consciously need to think about breathing, but you do expect to breathe.

Are you in fear of breathing? No, but you may be in fear of not breathing. Imagine your reaction when suddenly your oxygen supply is cut off; the only focus you have is on catching another breath.

But expectation does not need to be fearful. Expectation can be very empowering and positive. Herein lays a very important factor in becoming the best you can be.

If your expectations are driven by negative fear emotions rather than by positive reinforcing ones, you will marginalise your growth in whatever facet of your life these expectations remain.

Let's look at the breathing example to make this a little clearer. If you have a phobia about breathing (it is likely to be some form of claustrophobia), you may be able to pinpoint a time where you felt trapped, perhaps as a child or even later in life. It may be triggered by an episode of panic or some other traumatic experience.

I vividly recall a client of mine who was once stuck in an elevator and developed claustrophobia as a result. His reaction was that he felt suffocated and couldn't breathe. Although he understood that this was an irrational behaviour, it was nonetheless real to him. From that moment on, his expectation of getting into an elevator was to feel like he would be unable to breathe.

His physiological reaction to this was very distressing; he avoided elevators and instead always used the stairs, even in a twenty-story buildings. We could say that this also had a positive reinforcing effect, as it kept him rather fit.

That would be fine if it did not represent a negative motivational reinforcer: the fear and expectation of what would happen once inside the elevator.

Let's keep it simple, though, and continue at this stage with the work analogy.

If you go to your work, fearful of losing your job because it would mean you cannot provide for your family and protection of your safety needs and physiological needs, you may be more inclined to take less risks at work and be less inclined to look for opportunities elsewhere.

Where the extrinsic motivation of the job (the reward) takes precedent over the (intrinsic motivation) value of the work you are doing, negative motivational fear reinforcers drive the expectation of work.

If you look at work from another angle, where the value of the work is the motivator, this form of motivation is more than likely to be indicative of your intrinsic motivators, which will be positive. If your job is extrinsically motivating, you may develop wanderlust tendencies and eventually leave. If you are fearful of not getting another job, your expectation is that you will do all you can to keep the one you have, no matter how miserable it makes you because it serves a purpose that is greater than the alternative, which is an unknown.

By this reasoning, you won't know what will happen until it happens. The major problem with this is that you are likely to feel miserable until something does happen. At that point, there is a possibility that the result will have been negatively reinforced over time, and therefore the experience is likely to be negative.

Visualising a positive outcome by focusing on what you want from a job can turn the table on the result and offer a rewarding and positive experience. Importantly, you do not have to have specific job in mind at this stage. You need only focus on what an ideal job would provide you with.

> # There are two ways to be happy: improve your reality or lower your expectations.
> —Anon.

Okay, at this point, write down some ideas. I'll give you a few starters to consider. Under these headings, write down what each would look like; what would these things mean to you in an ideal job:

- reward

- recognition
- satisfaction

What do you expect from work? Make some notes about this now in your diary. It may not be in the job you are in; it may be your hypothetical dream job, if you have one. Let your imagination go here, as everything is possible in your mind if you can visualise it.

Now, extend this thought to other aspects of your life. What are your expectations with your family, friends, community groups, politicians, sports teams, and so on?

Example: Job

- Reward: I'd like a gift for my dedication and productivity.
- Recognition: I deserve a promotion for my hard work.
- Satisfaction: I want the opportunity to have my ideas considered.

You don't have to do all of this right now. This is an exercise that you can return to frequently, as ideas spring to mind.

This book is not a race; the only competitor here is you. The new you is competing with the old one. The better-equipped strategist always comes out on top, so take a little time.

Expectation

What Is the Expectation?	Certainty	Family	Work	Leisure	Overall Rating of Expectation
Will not get promotion	8	2	9	8	6.75

Let's look at another hypothetical situation with someone we'll identify as Jim.

Jim understands there is promotion opportunity at work. He is considering applying for it but is weighing up his chances of being successful.

Looking at the company's past record of promotion, he sees there is a trend to overlook internal applicants and promote the positions externally to inject new blood and ideas into the firm. Jim has applied for several other promotions and has been unsuccessful on each occasion. He has not asked why he was unsuccessful or how he could improve to increase his chances.

His expectation of failure is high. Why? We discuss this specifically in chapter 3, but it is clear that there is a valid reason for Jim's belief and his expectation of failure. It has happened before.

Looking deeper into the overall rating under this expectation, we can see what affects this result. Jim's family believes he is a good man, passionate about his job; he just needs the opportunity, in their eyes. His family is his support mechanism; however, when tempered with what he feels about past experiences and what he has accomplished in his job, he understands that he may not be the best candidate. He is aware of his shortfalls (or his perception of them).

How can Jim change this? Visualising what the ideal candidate would look like and making the necessary changes so that he becomes that candidate would certainly add to his chances. Homework, research, perhaps further study are all positive steps to increase his visibility and viability in the new role.

What are the negatives to reduce in order to promote his chances?

Jim has identified a strong negative factor against his promotion as his leisure activities.

How can this be a hindrance to his chances?

It's well known that Jim is an avid sports fan. Apart from playing team sports on Saturdays and regular Wednesday afternoon golf, he is the coach of the local basketball team on Tuesdays and Thursdays and travels with the team for their matches on Sundays. In addition, he is on the local PTA at his kids' school and is regularly involved in fundraising activities.

It is an unfortunate fact that many employers are aware of the extracurricular activities of their employees for a number of reasons. Could their activities have a detrimental effect on their work? Could there be a negative consequence to the company if some activities have a political aspect or some other strong divisive public opinion surrounding it? Could it hinder Jim's ability to perform outside of his normal work hours?

It is not that long ago that many multinational companies would regularly transfer their management staff to different locations to prevent them from engaging in too many community-based projects and thus deviate from their full attention to the company.

In this scenario, Jim still has a less than 50 percent belief that he will get the promotion. If he doesn't believe in himself, it is unlikely others will believe in him, either.

How can he improve on this so that his expectation falls into a very positive frame?

- Review past failures. What went wrong? Who got the job he didn't? What did they have he didn't?
- What area is the most positive encouragement coming from? We can see this is his family. We can include friends and acquaintances in this group. Jim should ask for a

warts-and-all opinion on what he has and doesn't have to succeed. A warning: Jim needs to be able to take the answers and responses on the chin. Negative opinion is as good or better than positive reporting. It forces you to analyse weaknesses and encourages you to improve.

- Talk to his managers. Request feedback on his work; ask about what may improve his chances.
- Indicate early his intentions and promote his successes.
- See what others who are successful in this position are doing.
- Critically review his qualifications for the position; what could he do to enhance this?
- Research the requirements and be prepared for positive answers. Most interviews these days will include questions on situations, actions, and outcomes. He can rehearse these and give direct answers, avoiding the urge to promote hypothetical situations. Employers want to know what he has done, not what he thinks he would do.
- Look for a mentor to help him.

Necessity

If you remember Maslow's hierarchy of needs, you may recall that you need very little in order to live. However, if you're like most people, you undoubtedly want to personalise your life, enjoy some comforts, experience some joy, and reduce stress.

What you perceive as necessary to you to live your life as you want is probably quite different from everyone else on the planet. Nevertheless, if you make something necessary to you and it is driven by the correct motivation, you will consistently make it happen.

Your life is driven by needs and the factors that influence them.

Needs are your perception of what is essential to exist and thrive. When your needs are not met, your fear level can be elevated.

Necessity is the third of your primordial drivers. At the safety and physiological needs level, of course, these things are obvious; to recap, they include food, water, shelter, and protection of what you hold dear to you.

Now, here is where you start to personalise your motivators.

What is necessary to you? What could you *not* do without? Why?

What you hold as precious is very individualised. This is important; it is often hard to comprehend what people are willing to defend. If you waste time on trying to understand everything that is important to others, you are only robbing yourself of time for self-reflection on your own needs, dreams, and aspirations.

I remember an episode of one of those survivor programmes on television. In this particular series, the contestants were not allowed any luxury items to take to their remote destination.

There were only a few people involved in the programme, and bearing in mind these contestants were to be exposed to very basic living conditions, one contestant needed her eyeliner. Realising that going without this was going to be a problem for her, she had her eyeliner tattooed on.

Apparently, naked and exposed was okay and acceptable, but being without eyeliner was not.

Necessity is defined as absolutely required for survival; clearly, in the example above, the need for eyeliner was seen as a necessity, right up there with food and water.

As Western culture has evolved, it poses an ever-increasing list of considerations of what you believe is necessary for your survival and continued existence; in fact, what is necessary for you to live in a Western society has increased at a staggering rate in the last decade alone.

Many businesses and organisations would founder or cease to exist if it were not for innovations in communication and information technology. You wouldn't really want to be a fax machine salesman right now, would you?

In the business example, the necessity to survive is to embrace new technology or become extinct.

At a personal level, technology has also made very intrusive inroads into our lives that have made owning devices such as laptop computers and cell phones almost mandatory for most people. These innovations are now a part of our lives and have become necessary to us. The last few generations have no idea of what life was like without these things.

In analysing what is necessary for you, it's important to look at exactly what we want you to consider. That is, those things that are necessary to you, which will include the following:

- **Must-haves.** What must you have at present? E.g. in your life work, play
- **Imperatives.** Without this, I would not be able to …
- Things that are **forced by compliance.** Vehicle registration, insurance, and so on.

Looking at yourself now, write what's necessary for you at this moment in your life. Record as many things as you can under as many headings as you can think of; remember this list should only be limited by your imagination.

You may wish to take some time and list your perceived necessities now.

I will present a case involving a necessity that many people rate highly.

Tony is a middle-aged middle-level executive in a very competitive industry. His lifestyle and family requirements dictate the amount of money he needs to earn to keep their heads above water. Fear of not being able to provide for them drives him to keep his head down and perform his job diligently. His expectation is that if he doesn't make waves, performs his duties, and receives favourable periodic reviews, he will continue to receive the remuneration that covers his needs.

Necessities

What Is the Necessity?	Certainty	Family	Work	Leisure	Overall Rating of Necessity
Money	10	8	10	5	8.25

Tony's first recording around necessity is related to money. The indicators are strong that money is his motivator; his reasoning suggests that this is an extrinsic motivator. The high recordings related to family and work confirm this is more likely extrinsic motivation. Why? Because when we look at his leisure rating, it is low. The leisure rating is the most personal rating. His score suggests that he doesn't require money to enjoy himself.

Nevertheless, the overall rating for money as a necessity remains high. Tony needs to ask these questions:

- How can he reduce the importance of money?
- If he is barely making ends meet, what can he do to reduce costs?

- What things that he thinks are necessary can he possibly do without?
- How would reducing costs affect what he sees as necessary?
- Alternatively, how could he make more money?
- What would more money do for him?
- Could he increase his income in his current position?
- Should he look for better prospects elsewhere?
- What has he got to offer that another employer would pay more for?
- Is he working in an extrinsically motivating job?

Clearly, comparing it with the other necessities, Tony's records may modify the initial item on his list (money) and its level of importance. This is best scrutinised under the onion principle. It requires a deal of reflection on each layer described under his necessities to ensure it leads to modification of his habits.

Take care of the luxuries and the necessities will take care of themselves.

—Dorothy Parker

Habit

The final driver is **habit**.

Changing habits is critical to move forward; it is the stumbling block many people fall over on when trying to achieve goals.

To be successful in making any change towards achieving goals and desires, it is absolutely necessary to analyse your habits and modify them, form new habits, or drop them altogether. An important fact is that time is a critical factor in life. Why would you waste any of it on unnecessary, routine, and mundane tasks that are a hindrance rather than assistance to you?

Keeping a daily diary of what you do for several weeks and then review it; you will see where you are wasting time and on what. You need to make a serious and conscious effort about the detail you record in your diary. The trick is to just write; don't analyse what you're writing or make sense of it. That comes later. For now, you just want a clinical record.

Habits can be good or bad for you. They can influence your behavioural changes or dissuade you from making them. Whatever; positive change requires positive action. Changing your habits is the key to that action.

I love Albert Einstein's definition of insanity: "doing the same thing over and over again and expecting different results." It sums up very succinctly the problems we have with habits.

This is so true, and yet you constantly experience people doing just this. You want to change something, but you don't want to do anything different to achieve it. You become ambivalent.

You say, "I want to, but I don't want to."

Why?

Well, you fear change because it may alter your expectation, and it isn't really necessary for you because there is no threat to your current needs. It's safer to stay in your perceived comfort zone.

By now, you should be recording your fears, expectations, and necessities; you are going to tie these things into your habits. If not, you may want to take a moment and go back and do it now.

Habit is how you identify yourself and how others identify with you. It adds further to your uniqueness and is an outward manifestation of who you are to others. It has reliability to it, and therefore, it sits comfortably. It can be very ritualistic and subconsciously driven.

As the old saying goes, "Habits die hard," and this is particularly true when you are considering any change in your behaviour.

The hardest thing you will have to do to become a better you is to change, alter, or discontinue your current habits. Like an addiction, they are very hard to let go of.

Why? Well, fear, for a starter.

If you consider changing a habit, you may become fearful of a degree of loss. However, it is important to realise that it is unlikely that changing a habit will affect either your safety or physiological needs.

What you are talking about here are the habits that fixate you at the current position you hold in life, work, and play. Going to a job you hate is a negatively reinforcing habit; staying in an unproductive relationship because of habit is also negatively reinforcing.

I want to make it clear that this is not a suggestion that when you review your habits, you should totally abandon your current job or relationship. It may be that after analysing your habits within those domains, there are changes you can make that will be beneficial to you (and possibly others) within that job or relationship that will make you a better you.

Challenging habits can be daunting, but it can also be a lot of fun.

The good thing about challenging habits is that it can be done without too much disruption. Remember that these are your habits, and they are there to be challenged by you. Others can certainly challenge you too; things like smoking and drinking excessively are two of society's challenges to an individual's habits.

These two examples show how both negative and positive reinforcers work.

By recognising habits and rituals, you can identify how and what you do consistently and continually. Upon reflection of your habits, you can understand why opportunities may not magnetise themselves to you initially and why you often don't get past the first hurdle when attempting to realise an opportunity and turn it into a goal.

- Eating fatty foods and consuming more calories than you burn will never make you lose weight.
- Thinking about starting something is of no value until you start it.
- Realising the benefits of ceasing a negative behaviour won't stop the behaviour.

Understanding that continuing in a job you hate or staying in a relationship that is not working for you won't make it better by merely understanding it. It requires action of some sort, which most likely insists that you change habits in one form or another.

What keeps you in your habitual routine is comfort.

Comfort merely means that the known is better than the unknown. You stick with what you know because at this point, it's easy. Note I did not say "ideal"; it's just that the fear and expectation of the known is more motivating to you. The unknown, on the other hand, may not be worth the risk at this point.

Why is it not worth the risk?

It comes back to your focus, your ideals, your intrinsic and extrinsic motivators. (At this point, I certainly hope you are defining what these motivators look like and mean to you.)

Where a current condition meets your extrinsic motivators, you may be inclined to accept it, even though deep down, you are aware that it's not ideal.

Examples of this are people who remain with a violent partner, or people who remain in jobs that are demeaning. Why do they do this? Because there is an expectation that this is what they deserve, and anything else may be worse. Besides, it is sufficiently satisfying to meet their extrinsic motivation and at least some of their needs. In other words, the behaviour is a negative reinforcer.

Statistically, people leaving a violent relationship are more likely to enter into another violent relationship.

Why? Because of habit.

This self-flagellating behaviour is negatively reinforced perhaps because of the internal conflict between your adult and your child. In this case, the disparity between these two parts of the psyche may be too great to be moderated by the conscience to enable you to visualise anything different.

The separation from the situation and the new environment may produce anxiety, causing reflection on the positive elements of the relationship, even though the negative outweighs them.

The recognition of the positive and known elements from the previous relationship are attractive enough to disregard the possibility of any negative elements recurring. In order to see how habits can influence you, we need to critically evaluate what things you do consistently and how they appear necessary to ensure your expectations are met and your fears are alleviated.

Ritualistic behaviour protects you in a number of ways. If your expectation is that if you go to work you will get a paycheck, which in turn will meet your financial needs in order to pay your bills, feed your family, and provide a roof over your head, then you will habitually go to work.

If you are watching your food intake and regularly exercise, the likelihood of success with the regime becoming a habit is directly proportional to how successful the actions are in maintaining the goal, which is to maintain a healthy weight and a fit body.

Where you engage in behaviour that regularly and consistently provides what you expect from it, you will habitually perform it. Most of your habits are of such longevity that they have become subconscious actions.

Evaluating and changing or eliminating habits that may prevent you from achieving a new goal can be a difficult process if the habit fulfils some positive reinforcement or provides some level of enjoyment.

In another hypothetical case, let's look at Jill.

Jill has a smoking habit.

Jill is a busy legal executive, which adds considerable stress and anxiety to her life. Smoking is a particularly difficult habit to break (although it is a fairly lucrative source of income for various cessation programmes and products). While many of these assistance programmes work, the level of effectiveness is directly proportional to the motivation the person has to quit.

Why is it so difficult?

Well, smoking is more than just a habit; it is an addiction. A big problem is that the brain recognises nicotine, as we are born with nicotinic receptors (meaning our system recognises it and accepts it).

Smokers will usually tell you they generally feel good about smoking. It provides a stress relief, calms their nerves, pacifies them, and a number of other credible reactions.

This makes breaking the habit exceptionally difficult. In this case, we are asking Jill to give up something that is positively reinforcing to her. In order to change this behaviour and quit the habit, there needs to be a stronger and more intrinsic motivation to take its place.

Reasons for quitting are well-documented. Lessening the potential for lung disease and cancers, cost, and social acceptability are all promoted as valid reasons to quit; however, unless aligned to an immediate need and personalised to an individual, they are extrinsic motivators and probably destined to fail.

When weighed against the benefits the smoker gets from maintaining the behaviour, we will undoubtedly have an internal conflict on our hands. At this stage, we have all of the benefits Jill gets from maintaining the behaviour measured only against the generic rationale for quitting.

Habit

Habit	Frequency	Family	Work	Leisure	Overall Frequency
Smoking	9	8	8	9	8.5

Jill's smoking is a frequent habit. At home, it is accepted, as her husband is a smoker, as well; due in part to the stress of her work, she is exposed to more smokers, leaving Jill with a fairly entrenched habit with little or no reason to change it.

Lately, due to the regulations disallowing smoking in the work place, Jill and her colleagues are forced to take smoking breaks in designated areas. Rather than discourage smoking, this has had a reinforcing impact on Jill, as the smoking becomes in part a social interaction with her colleagues.

In her leisure environment, Jill enjoys playing cards with her and her partner's friends, who are all smokers.

We can see that the habit remains very strong, primarily because there is no reason to cease that is motivating enough. While all the health and cost benefits are valid (negative perspectives), they have not had an impact on Jill (yet) and so are outweighed by the positive reinforcers.

The answer to changing the habit is to consider another activity where smoking would have a negative consequence to it. The activity would need to be intrinsically motivating enough for Jill to consider changing her habit.

Habits are what will make your journey to achieving desires and goals a success or a failure. It is habits that got you to where you are now, and you have identified that where you are is not where you want to be. Changing habits, therefore, is imperative to get you where you want to be. As habits are deeply engrained in your current behaviour, the hardest thing you will have to do is to ensure you change them and that they stay under constant surveillance and review.

We are what we repeatedly do. Excellence, then, is not an act but a habit.

—Douglas McArthur

3

The Four Rs of Failure

Reluctance, Rebellious, Rationalising, and Resigned

The Four Failure Indicators

Failure indicators are a realistic look at why you may have failed in previous attempts at making changes in your life or why you have never achieved your dreams, goals, and desires.

The indicators fall into four categories. Generally, failure will be as a result of more than one of these working in tandem, or you may fail through a series of issues that follow sequentially. Nevertheless, you will be able understand your failures by the indicators outlined below.

The failure indicators are there for you to see in your everyday experiences, just like a maintenance programme for your vehicle. Check your reasoning for not changing an habitual behaviour that you know is working against you; the following four groups explain why you have failed and why you will continue to fail, if these indicators are present.

The Four Rs of Failure

1. Reluctance (discomfort with a situation or process)

When you are reluctant to do something, it is because you have had a negative experience with the situation or a process that was similar to the current one was unpleasant. Your perception of the situation may be negative. Perception can be a result of those annoying schema we talked about, or it may be because others give you a rendition of their experience with a similar situation.

Remember that despite the good intentions of others, their experiences will not be the same as yours. It is important to weigh up fact from fiction and analyse how the situation could be changed to meet your needs.

Discomfort is not as strong an emotion as feeling uncomfortable or, worse, unbearable.

If something is a discomfort to you, it may be annoying, but if it does not radically affect your expectations, you may accept it.

Take, for example, a demanding boss. There may be veiled threats about staff performance to encourage better work ethics; this is a negative reinforcer. However, unless the behaviour increases and becomes personal to you, you are unlikely to do anything about it.

If you find you are reluctant in some aspects of your life, this is an early warning sign that you need to review where you are going and what is impeding your progress.

If your failure to make change is due to reluctance, it may suggest that your fear of failure is greater than your expectation for success.

To avoid this failure indicator, take time to start formalising some goals and putting some time frames around them. Critically evaluate the level of intrinsic motivation that your ideas meet.

2. Rebellion

When failure is a result of a rebellious action, this is often an example of cutting off your nose to spite your face. In the seventeenth century, Blaise Pascal stated that "we are generally persuaded by reasons we have ourselves discovered than by those that have occurred to others." In other words, when others make decisions about what you should be doing, you often rebel against that suggestion.

Backing Off/Counteraggressive

Born from frustration, there is a natural tendency to rebel against people's actions that do not fit with your way of thinking. These things often become unbearable and keep you from attempting to change.

Your actions may manifest in poor performance, deliberate sabotage, and a pattern of blaming.

A pattern of rebellion often occurs because you feel marginalised in some way. There is a tendency to blame others for your failures while at the same time recognising that you are the orchestrator of your own life. Blaming others is actually a sign of a lack of commitment to change.

If you recognise this in your actions, it is a sign there are problems brewing and it's time to do something about it. Internalising this behaviour and acting negatively can affect your personal relationships, your work, and your health.

Falling into the trap of this failure indicator will be recognised by those close to you, so take heed if friends or family make comments about your behaviour.

3. Rationalising

Rationalising essentially means finding a way to quit (or to not get started in the first place). You can convince yourself by coming up with reasons why something won't work for you. With the benefit of websites like Google, you can find well-meaning articles that confirm your rationalising beliefs to prove to yourself and others why something won't work for you.

In researching something, you are likely to find as many opinions supporting an activity as there are that don't. It is for you to decide whether the action you are considering is the right fit for you. If the situation is unpleasant, consider whether it is necessary to gain the goal you desire. If motivation towards the end goal is intrinsic and strong enough, you will find a way to get through any interim processes towards achieving it.

Impatience

If you can identify with a rationalising behaviour and feel you are becoming impatient, you run the risk of accepting less than you desire.

The net result of this behaviour may be a sudden, knee-jerk reaction to any experience that is less than satisfactory. You may be unhappy in your job, in your relationship, or with your health and fitness.

An example of rationalising behaviour around fitness and health is where you say, "I can't change this; I was born with it. I've tried the gym and diet before; it doesn't work. I may as well just camp on the couch and eat pizza."

Suddenly, that seems like an appropriate course of action. You've rationalised a behaviour that you *know* is not good for you, but it feels good at the moment because you have tried and failed at achieving the alternative. Rationalising is born from frustration.

This is also a clear example of where motivation is a state, not a trait. It also identifies the difference between possible amotivation (couch, movie, and pizza) over an intrinsic motivator (be healthy and fit).

If you fall into this failure mode, it may be because you haven't established goals for yourself that allow you to look past the extrinsic motivators (the actual actions to get you fit and healthy). You may be setting your goals too high, without a clear vision of what being healthy and fit will do for you.

If you make goals attainable and then pursue them, you will be guaranteed not to fall into the rationalising trap. Decide why you want to achieve these goals first. Strengthen your motivation; your behaviour will adapt accordingly.

4. Resignation

Resignation is explained by the psychological condition known as learned helplessness. Learned helplessness describes how an organism learns to accept and endure unpleasant stimuli, even when they are avoidable.

Hopelessness

If you get trapped by this failure mechanism, you are likely to have already followed the pathway from the other three.

But it's not a lost cause; you can also shake off the shackles of helplessness by reviewing your needs and analysing how your current behaviour may have an effect on them.

Hopelessness is also a warning that you may be heading towards a state of amotivation, which can have a detrimental effect on your health and well-being.

People generally feel helpless when their power to make decisions is removed from them; this is only a perception, and when you look closely, you often find your position is one you've allowed to happen.

The pathway to hopelessness can be very slow and insidious, driven by a series of negatively impacting events that serve to only increase your fear and expectation that this negativity will continue.

Once again, the notoriously mischievous schema may be the culprit. If you experience this type of failure, it is time to analyse the negative perceptions that you have within your onion that are holding you back. Take some time to deliberately challenge these preconceived ideas. Monitor how these feelings of negativity affect you. One of the classic features of depression and anxiety is the feeling of helplessness. If this happens to you, you need to have faith in your mentor. If you don't have one, then it is time to find one.

Giving up on your goal is like slashing your other three tires because you got a flat.
—Anon.

4

Two Essential Ingredients: Importance and Confidence

Two Essential Ingredients

To put it bluntly as possible, if something isn't important to you, it is unlikely you will do it (at least not to the extent that you would if was stimulating intrinsically motivating and provided a positive end result). Before finalising any action towards a behavioural change, you must determine just how important something is to you. If the level of importance is low, it may be because you feel you don't have the necessary skills, time, or resources to be successful. If that is the case, it's time to review your weaknesses under your level of perceived ability.

Remember that if desire, need, and reason can be established strongly, this will help resolve the issue of ability. Understanding the process of reviewing the importance of a behaviour as outlined below will identify the true level of importance to you.

Importance and confidence are your personal measurement guides; they act as a visual perception of the level of importance and confidence you have in achieving your desires.

These two ingredients are essential to identifying your goals and achieving them. If your importance is high and your confidence is low, the first step is to improve your confidence. You need to know where the confidence you have comes from and expand on it.

If your importance is low but your confidence is high, perhaps you have not defined your desire clearly enough; you need to review the desire more clearly.

In order to make the best of the programme outlined in this book and in making you the best you can be, you must continuously review how well you are doing, which means asking yourself these questions every week:

- Is this goal still important to me?
- Do I want to modify it in any way?
- Am I still on track?
- What success have I achieved so far?
- Is my confidence still strong?
- What is influencing me at this very moment?

Also ask yourself the same questions related to how confident you are that you are on track. What gives you this confidence? Are you increasing in confidence? Why?

(Name a goal or make a list of goals at this point if you can.)

To indicate why you desire something and how confident you are in achieving it, test your motivation towards realising it and analyse your strengths and weaknesses.

It helps to visualise this on a scale from 0 to 10, where 0 indicates absolutely no importance or confidence and 10 indicates absolute importance or confidence.

Importance
0-----1-----2-----3-----4-----5-----6-----7-----8-----9-----10

Confidence
0-----1-----2-----3-----4-----5-----6-----7-----8-----9-----10

When you are considering engaging in behaviour towards achieving a goal, draw up two rulers as indicated above.

Take a pen and circle your rating in each domain of importance and confidence.

To give you an example of how this works, let's consider Scott.

Scott would like to be self-employed. He has no idea how to set up a business and has no experience running one. He has worked solidly and effectively for his current employer, his previous employers all regarded him as a valuable employee who contributed significantly to the success of their business.

Having looked at his history and achievements, he realises that he no longer gains any satisfaction from being an employee. In the past, he has chosen to change his work environment for stimulation, but now he wants something more.

Understanding his motivation to improve himself, he reasons that the challenge of making all of the decisions appeals to him; he also understands that there may be some pitfalls along the way, including some financial issues. His income may decrease in the short term. He will spend more time promoting his business on top of the time he needs to actually work; his family and friends need to understand he will not be as available as he was.

In relation to the business itself, he has a working knowledge of pricing and accounting, as he has already had some exposure to these things from his employers. However, he needs to establish a line of credit from his bank, buy insurance, and learn how to employ staff.

Scott has researched all of these processes on line and believes he can handle them all; where he is limited in expertise, he has searched for help in these areas and has found several websites that specialise in assisting new businesses.

In addition to a totally new business venture, Scott has also explored the possibility of a franchise operation, where he could be self-employed but with help from a franchisor in finding new work, accounting and advertising assistance, and promoting his business.

He's now ready to take the plunge, but before he does, he wants to consider what he hopes to get out of his business. Is he venturing into an area that is important enough to meet his expectations? Is he confident enough that he has the skills, motivation, and desire to succeed?

Importance

Situation	Idea	Work	Family	Leisure	Overall
Self-employment	7	9	8	8	8

On a scale of overall importance, Scott's score registers high at 8.

At this point, you may consider that the strength of importance is not high enough. You might consider that the only acceptable level for a decision like this should be an emphatic 10.

Not necessarily so. 10 may indicate that the importance level suggests a need to urgently get out of the current situation at any cost; however, we have established that Scott has enjoyed his employment and his employer. His need is presented as a requirement to gain something more than what being an employee can provide for him.

If you looked at Scott's needs, you would find that his current situation provides for the majority of them. The things he has not achieved are things he has not experienced, so there will be some softening of the importance, and that is to be expected.

To understand the level of importance and thereby solidify his reasons to become his own boss, you would ask Scott, "You have indicated that the importance to you of self-employment on a scale of 0–10 is on average 8; tell us why it is not, say, 6?"

Scott's response can be one of two things.

Firstly, he can both explain why it is not 6 and confirm his score of 8. If this is his response, the confirmation will describe why his level of importance is greater than 6.

If you were to ask him why he is not a 10, his response would most likely indicate all of the negative reasons for his response given as an 8.

Secondly, he could respond with, "You're right; that's a bit ambitious. I'm actually more of a 6."

Presented with this response, you might ask, "Why then are you not a 4?"

This process not only gives you a true indicator of the importance to you but also the true identification of your reasons, strengths, and weaknesses.

The next phase is to test confidence, using the same format.

If it's important to you, you'll find a way; if it isn't, you'll find an excuse.

—Anon.

Confidence

Confidence is measured on the same scale as we measure importance.

What is confidence? It is a measure of belief in your ability to perform any given task at any given moment. Like motivation, confidence is a state, not a trait. By making behavioural changes, you need to increase your level of confidence in maintaining those changes until they become subconscious habits.

Just as in the process of reviewing importance, review the level of confidence to understand the reasons for that confidence. It is not to describe the rationale for any perceived lack of confidence, which would only serve to create negativity and return you to the four reasons for failure.

Confidence

Situation	Idea	Work	Family	Leisure	Overall
Self-employment	4	4	5	3	4

Scott's score of overall confidence registers low, at an overall rating of 4.

Using the same format of questioning, you would ask Scott, "Why are you not at a 2 or 3 in your confidence?"

While the score may be low, there are a number of variables to account for this. Even the most confident people are inclined to question their ability, to a degree. Using this format, you can only reason why your confidence is greater than a 2 by discussing the positive aspects of your confidence.

By his own explanation, Scott is telling himself that he has some genuine reasons to be confident.

At this point, you have established Scott's level of validity for how important this decision is for him and also his level of confidence.

Scott will have identified his fears, expectations, necessities, and habits; he has determined how these will impact his importance and confidence.

All of the hypothetical candidates I have identified previously will have followed all of the stages described within these chapters.

In order to further establish their motivation and put some real tangible interventions to their plans to enable change, Annie, Jim, Tony, Jill, and Scott must now identify the strengths and weaknesses of their ability to realise their goals.

The following chapter investigates the desires they have to achieve their goal, their ability to make the changes necessary and evaluate the need to make these changes, and finally their reason for wanting to make them.

Confidence is like a muscle: the more you use it, the stronger it gets.
—Anon.

5

The Four Change Indicators: Desire, Ability, Reason, and Need

The Four Change Indicators

How do you know what your goals are?

You are going to start to use this programme to identify your goals and determine the tools and interventions you need to achieve them.

1. **Desire: You want something because ...**
2. **Ability: You can make it happen because ...**
3. **Reason: It would help you if you had it because ...**
4. **Need: You need it because ...**

The most valuable of all education is the ability to make yourself do the thing you have to do, when it has to be done, whether you like it or not.
—Aldous Huxley

Desire

Throughout this book, I have interchanged the word *desire* with *goal*. Essentially, desire is the umbrella that all goals fit under. You may need to reach a number of goals before attaining your ultimate desire.

The reason desire is not the only reference is that for many people, what begins as an absolute desire and a concentrated focus may change as they define and refine what the real desire looks like in the end. This may be a subtle change, such as the colour of a vehicle you desire, or it may be a complete paradigm shift from what you first envisioned.

While desire is the ultimate goal, you should view intermediate goals as victories. Turning desires into reality, as the subtitle of this book suggests, is not only about gaining something you desire but also enjoying and growing from the experience along the way to achieving it.

Desire is a strong and emotive expression of what you want; it evokes the expectation of a positive experience. Desires are linked to your intrinsic motivators.

In order to test the true level of the desire you identify, you must clearly understand what it is and be able to communicate it and review your ability to achieve it. Exploring needs and identifying desires in context with the requirements to turn them into reality give purpose to the steps necessary to make the desire realistically attainable.

The object of desire should be physically or mentally possible to achieve. If you are less than 160 centimetres tall and desire to be taller than 180, you might be disappointed.

Realising that gaining height is impossible for you may prevent you from exploring alternatives that may achieve the same result. For example, if you want to gain height to make you a better basketball player, perhaps the real intrinsic motivator is being a better basketball player.

When you look harder, you might find that your reasons will make this clearer. You approach change through your strongest support mechanisms. If being taller is the initial desire, the new desire may be a modification of that need.

If it fits with your perception of what you envision a better basketball player can do because he is taller, you need to look at what added height provides. Being taller may not bring with it the other requirements that you already have, such as scoring ability or defensive prowess.

Being taller is an advantage in this context, but so too are speed, fitness, dexterity, and determination; without those components, height on its own does not guarantee being better.

If you investigate the potential with the tools and abilities you have in the other areas, perhaps you could improve your performance playing basketball.

However, if the sense of futility is so great and the whole idea of being a taller basketball player is dismissed, there are still ways to identify pursuits that could be equally desirable, once you investigate what you expected your original desire to provide.

Things are not always as cut and dried as you first think. Falling at the first hurdle is common. Setting unrealistic goals can kill motivation from the outset.

Many goals and inspirations are stymied by the "yes … but" and "If only …" responses. When questioned about why you are not progressing towards your goal, if you begin with these statements, you are already subjecting yourself to failure and building hurdles that may actually not be there.

Being too rigid at the beginning can also lead to disappointment. When working towards achieving a desire, think of the desire in broader terms. Envisage a funnel, and imagine throwing all the elements of desire into the top.

As you gain more information and begin to formulate a clearer picture of the desire, your vision may change as the knowledge you gain gets filtered through the funnel.

What comes out may not even resemble what you put in.

It's an exciting process and full of surprises, but what you ultimately present will be uniquely personalised to you and your overall desire.

What that desire is in tangible terms will be much clearer. Importantly, it will include support mechanisms you already have and perhaps didn't know how to use. These support mechanisms will ensure you have the best possible chance of achieving the core rationale for your desire.

When we start looking at our desires, we should see them as an open book, a proverbial wish list without boundaries.

Viewing what you desire by using visual images, writing and reading about them, and adding to the information you have are important to maintain the motivation that keeps you going.

Keep thinking about your desires; place photos on the wall, beside your mirror, or around your desk. Write them down in a list; enter as many desires as you like. In fact, the more the merrier. Don't be afraid to add ones that may seem far-fetched, too grand, too expensive, or too complex. The more you have, the more likely you are to ensure you will be focussed on what you really want. You will eventually filter these into a tangible and attainable direction that will be intrinsically motivating.

One of the most rewarding aspects of this process is looking back on where you have come from and seeing where you are headed. The feeling of accomplishment is a strong motivator in itself and provides the incentive to test what else you are capable of.

We will continue with examples through the other elements of DARN to explain this concept fully as we progress.

Let's present another hypothetical situation.

Les is fixated with changing his job; it occupies much of his thoughts throughout the day. He is losing sleep and worrying about his situation.

It is time he did something about it.

Desire

Goal	Strength of Desire	Family	Work	Leisure	Overall Level of Desire
New job. I really want a change of scenery.	9 If I don't get a job I feel valued in, I will go deeper into depression.	9 I'm unhappy where I am; it takes its toll on the rest of my life and those I care about.	7 The job I have pays me what I need; money isn't my prime mover.	9 If I had a new job, I could get out and about more and do the things I enjoy doing, and that is extremely important to me.	8.5 I really want a new job; it is the most important thing to me at the moment.

In this instance, Les has identified his desire as getting a new job.

The strength of the desire is high at 9; it relates equally high with his perception related to his family and leisure, with a slightly lower rating against work itself.

The language used is strong; it indicates that this is a priority for him.

We then take these same desires and post them against three other factors for consideration: ability, reason, and need.

While the overall rating for desire is high, there are some red flags. A lot of what Les has described is circumspect. There are no specifics to the hypothetical new position.

"Change of scenery" and "getting out and about" are not concrete enough to really describe an intrinsic desire to change jobs. You would expect a descriptive comparison of the current scenery with the desired scenery and how a fuller explanation around what getting out and about would look like and what more it would do for him.

The cursory description given suggests a frustration with the situation in his current position, perhaps best described as boredom. Look deeply at the motivation around the desires; is it possible that the desire he seeks can be obtained by modifying his present position?

By following through the process I describe, analysing his ability to orchestrate change in his current position and his reasons to change, you can determine with some degree of accuracy whether the decision to change jobs meets with his desires or whether the desire he seeks is available with some changes in his current position.

Your desire to change must be greater than your desire to stay the same.

—Anon.

Ability

Ability is a tricky one.

While the desire may be high, your ability to achieve it may seem to be low.

By far the biggest reason people fail at achieving even the simplest goal is their inability to do so (or, rather, their perception of their ability).

Stevie Wonder once said, "We all have the ability; the difference is in how we use it."

Your ability may surprise you; when motivation, need, fear, or any combination of these is high, your ability will come to the fore. In this chapter, we discuss recognising your ability and learning how to increase it using various sources. If you perceive a lack ability in a specific area, you should analyse who has that ability and can help you develop it.

At this point, it is about increasing ability and understanding of what you require. There are numerous sources these days; websites can point you in the right direction for almost everything, as long as you know what to ask.

You may be unaware of just what abilities you do have. Many people have hidden talents; take programs like *American Idol* or *Britain's Got Talent,* for example. A mild-mannered Scottish singer walks tentatively out onto a brightly lit stage about to turn her shower rendition of "I Dreamed a Dream" into a full-blown orchestral production, subjected to harsh criticism not only by a panel of judges but by millions of armchair critics around the world.

The result?

Wow, she could sing. The accolades (and millions of dollars) that flowed in certainly warranted the risk and the possibility of failure; after all, what was the worst that could have happened to Susan Boyle?

Still, there remains an element of self-doubt within most of us; the only real way to find out what you have is to look at the challenge and evaluate your actions on the probability that you can succeed. If not, what are the consequences of failure?

If you analyse your position and break the elements of the task into components, you can calculate your chances of success with a degree of certainty.

Importantly, if you come to the realisation that you lack ability in a necessary area, you can then shift the focus and investigate how to improve your ability in that area.

Firstly, you could identify who has what you need. Can you call on this person as a reliable resource?

Satisfying your ability does not mean you have to be the head cook and chief dishwasher too. Delegation, purchase of services, training sessions, and myriad other helpers are out there to boost your ability.

Using media resources, looking for a similar project; study their processes or pick their brains and find a mentor with experience in what you seek; these strategies can all increase your abilities. (Your ability in this context is to find them and use them.)

For this part of your examination into the process of turning a desire into reality, you need to be realistic. The words *might*, *maybe*, or *perhaps* are not strong enough language to drive you; there is an element of doubt echoing within them.

Similarly, contingency suggestions are unhelpful unless you go back and ensure the element of success is better than that of failure. The use of phrases such as "If X happens, then Y might work" are not motivating enough, unless you get a better idea of what X and Y are.

This is not to say that before venturing into a project, you must be 100 percent certain of success. Weighing positives against negatives should tell you that there is a more likely chance of success than not.

The biggest barrier to moving towards gaining what we desire is our perception of our ability to do so.
—Anon.

Once you are satisfied that you either have the ability or at least can improve as you go along, you are on your way.

Let's look at another scenario to see how ability can be assessed and challenged.

We'll stick with Les and his desire for a new job.

Perception of his ability in this example has taken a hit. The low recording may be because he has tried and failed several times.

There is limited resource available from family; slightly less is available from previous work or work influences, and the leisure aspects of his CV are perceived of little assistance.

Okay, no problem; you have merely defined a level of perception, not an actual true recording, at least not until you've explored his reasons for his new job.

Ability

Object of Desire	Ability to Achieve	Family	Work	Leisure	Overall Level of Ability
New job. However, there aren't many jobs available in my field around here.	5 I thought I was well qualified, but I'm concerned others have more ability than I have.	5 I have no one close to me who can assist me.	4 I have no contacts that can open doors for me.	2 My leisure interests do not enhance my CV.	4 I have little confidence in the opportunities available to me, and there is no one to give me advice or direction.

Les's overall self-assessment of his ability is low, rated at 4.

He seems to be addressing all the things he doesn't have, rather than looking at what he has. After a first glance at these recordings, you may question the overall desire to change jobs completely; it may indicate he is stale in his position, and his desire is more stimulation from his work.

The recordings are negative reinforcers. Lack of opportunity in his field suggests that it is not the type of work he wishes to change. His concern that he is less qualified than others may indicate he wants to shift before he gets shoved.

He has a perception that he has no familial support or business contacts to assist him; his leisure interests appear not to offer any promotion for him either. In this context, leisure activities often open the doors to other opportunities.

The language used is strongly negative; it consists of a lot of "nos" and "nots." These responses indicate that while Les has identified his desire, his review of his ability suggest the likelihood of him achieving it is remote.

This should not be viewed as a reason to abandon his idea; it merely indicates that ability is a weak area that requires more attention.

The key to the ability component is to take a good hard look at generic abilities. These can be strengthened by investigation into reasons and needs.

Ability is the strongest negative aspect in most endeavours to change in order to attain goals and desires. As stated earlier, the perception of a lack of ability is a stumbling block, preventing success. The primary reason for this is that the change required is often something you have never experienced. If you haven't done something, how do you know what to do?

Increasing ability is the key to success, but this doesn't necessarily mean hours of study or practice; it may mean you find people to help you achieve your goal. This could be purchasing a service, getting advice from a knowledgeable mentor, searching the web, or accessing other resources at your disposal. It simply means you have to ask and to look.

Reason

"My desire will help me by …"

Reasons add strength and a sense of purpose to a desire. They begin to personalise the benefits to you in real terms that can be identified, visualised, and verbalised.

Reasons are understood in terms of how the desire will help you.

You must answer this question: "If I achieved this desire, how would it help me?" Now start writing. As in the scenario below, there are myriad reasons for putting effort into something. As long as the motivation is intrinsic and strong, there is absolutely no reason why you cannot achieve it.

The purpose of this book is to increase your understanding of the process. In the scenarios presented, I have limited possible variables to specific areas of work, family, and leisure; however, these areas can be expanded on under more headings or further expanded under the ones you've recorded here.

Adding strengthening subjective comments in your reasoning makes explanation easier and helps you understand your plan.

It is easier for others (say, a bank manager who could offer you a loan) to assist you when they are able to identify clearly what you're trying to accomplish. If they can identify with what you want and why you want it, they are likely to be more constructive with their advice.

Reasoning explains your motives for your desire; the more you can record, the more critical analysis you can apply to ascertain the strength of your motivation.

Reasons give endorsement to the potential benefits you will gain from achieving your desired goal and clarify if they are intrinsically or extrinsically driven.

Let's imagine your desire is to gain a postgraduate degree. How would this benefit you?

Your reason list may include these comments:

- I like the intellectual stimulus I get from studying.
- It would enhance my CV.
- I have the time to do it now.
- I am really interested in expanding my knowledge in this area.
- My employer is encouraging me and financially supporting me.

In the reason area, you want to put forward positive statements; sure, there may be negatives weighing against the decision. You will be able to address those elements when you finalise your DARN programme.

Recording positive and negative reasons together at this stage increases the possibility of ambivalence; if that happens, it may be difficult to move forward. Bear in mind the process of DARN promotes what is positive. The language you use indicates the power of the positive motivation and identifies under what umbrella (intrinsic or extrinsic) it is coming from.

Later, when you have a clearer definition of your desire after examining reasons and needs, you can address any negative potentials through your Commitment, Action, and Taking Steps (CAT).

Keeping with Les, you understand that his idea of a new job rates top marks in desire for a reason. He has presented a number of variables, singularly and collectively.

Stronger indications of desire around employment would be where you may not have a job or are in a terrible job; however, if that is the case, the motivation may be more extrinsic. A job, perhaps any job, would suffice.

If this is the case, remember again that motivation is a state, not a trait, and the desire maybe a short-term objective rather than a life sentence.

Remember that reasons are more constructive and robust when they come from a positive perspective of what you will gain from the desire.

When you look at Les's recordings for reasons, he indicates his overall reasoning would suggest the current work environment is less than attractive.

Les wants to change a negative situation into a positive situation by considering a hypothetical positive outcome.

Reason

Goal	Strength of Reason	Family	Work	Leisure	Overall Strength of Reason
New job. If I have a new job, I won't have to put up with the environment I work in.	10 I hate this job. The management do not recognise my efforts, and I'm bored with the lack of challenge.	9 If I stay here, I will be impossible to be around because my negativity will pass onto others.	6 The work itself pays well. I just need to do it somewhere else with different people who appreciate me.	8 I don't want to wind up without a job; I have my leisure interests, which keep me going, and I need the money for them.	8.25 If I don't change jobs, I will focus only on the negative and become harder to be around as well as unhappy in myself.

The language Les uses in his reasoning is strongly negative. The use of phrases such as "hate," "bored," and "lack of recognition" indicate that he may make the rash decision to leave his job, but there are no jobs available in his location.

As far as family (this relates to your home environment), Les's reasoning is positive. However, when we look at where this motivation comes from, it is clearly external (it will be of benefit to his friends and family); he realises that his current behaviour is detrimental to his relationships, and it is situational (he sees his job and the problems he feels are impacting negatively on his behaviour towards friends and family).

Les sees he has the potential to be not nice to be around. His desire is driven in order to avoid a negative consequence. This suggests a strong extrinsic motivator towards his desire.

It dips a bit as far as his actual work goes, which means it may be the current environment he's in that is the problem rather than the job itself. He confirms this when he says he wants more appreciation for what he does.

Les clearly has some reservations about the effect of change on his leisure activities. Again, his reasons are extrinsic. Money is the motivator, as it is a requirement to maintain his leisure interests.

The final overall reasoning is high; however, it does cast some doubt on the strength of the desired goal of changing jobs. So far, your analysis suggests the real desire may be to modify his current job or gain more appreciation from it.

The level of enjoyment Les gains from his present work situation is so low that it's impacting his ability to engage in leisure activities, or they no longer give him pleasure because of the distraction of his current situation.

So his reasons are strong; that gives us direction. However, they appear to be strongly negatively reinforced and extrinsically motivated. Defining how severe the negative situation is and whether he can salvage the current situation or endorse the desire for a new job will become a bit clearer when you analyse Les's needs.

As can be seen in these hypothetical situations, the reason to do one thing may in fact support a stronger reason to do something else. However, by using this process, the actual reason that will provide a stronger motivation (and therefore a greater chance of success and happiness) will be evident. As I stated before, the process of change and goal setting should be flexible rather than a rigid life sentence. Be prepared to evaluate your findings, moderate or modify your goals, take time to evaluate your findings, and strengthen your abilities.

The minute you think of giving up, think of the reason you have held on.
—Anon.

Need

Now you are looking at some serious stuff.

Your question to yourself is now, "Why do I need this?" It's all very well to establish a desire and decide you have the ability to achieve it; even having a reason, however, does not necessarily mean you have strong enough motivation to get moving on it. Remember the chapter on importance and confidence?

Need brings you right back to those primordial drivers: your fear. What will happen if you don't get moving on achieving these goals? Your expectations: What can you expect if you don't make this change that would better for you? Your habits: How would changing some habits affect you? Sometimes, the thought of letting go of something is too much to consider, and therefore the need to maintain the status quo is more desirable. And finally, of course, there is necessity: Do you really need to do this? Write down all the reasons why you need to seek and attain this desire.

When you investigated and rated your necessities under the four primordial drivers, you were looking at what was necessary to maintain your status quo.

In this section, you are identifying what changes you need to make in order to achieve your desire and determining what those changes will do for you.

Needs indicate that you are stating, "This is really important to me." Achieving your goal takes precedence over everything else.

You are expressing the negative consequence of inaction and the expectation of positive action. Expressing your needs clearly signals that the desire you have is strong; it has tangible elements related to real situations, and it is intrinsically motivating.

The impact of achieving your desire and a clear vision of the effect that will have on you becomes clearer. It may also provide you with a series of required steps towards achieving what you are after and show how you can implement this.

Setting workable and reasonable time frames around your actions is the next phase.

Any plan to achieve a desire can be fraught with hiccups and hurdles. If your programme takes a setback, review your reasons and needs. As I have said many times before, motivation is a state, not a trait.

Most successful people will happily tell their story of the times they felt like giving up before regrouping and moving on again. It's a natural human reaction to occasionally have doubts. The sign of true intrinsic motivation is overcoming those doubts.

Recording needs expresses what will happen if you don't achieve your desire and reminds you of the objective, not the path to it.

Let's look at Les's needs and see what he considers important to him above all else.

All need indicators are high, so clearly this is pressing on his mind and absorbing a fair amount of attention from his thoughts.

Les has established, through the reasons he recorded, that his job is a problem, and it needs to be addressed. He has grave doubts over his ability; his reasons are negatively and extrinsically motivated.

Whatever the eventual direction he takes, it is clear that something should be done to change things for him.

He indicates the object of his desire is still a new job. The pressing element defined within his recorded needs is that without a job, he will be financially compromised.

Okay, this could be avoided by staying in his current position; however, his need is further strengthened considerably, as he is unhappy, and it's having an effect on his home life, as well.

Need

Goal	Strength of Need	Family	Work	Leisure	Overall Strength of Need
New job	9 If I don't change, I will be financially in trouble.	9 I need to change because I'm unhappy doing this, and it is affecting my home life.	10 I am better than this, and I have not fulfilled my potential where I am.	9 While I feel like this, I can't enjoy anything I used to.	9.25 I need to do this to feel confident in myself and rewarded by what I do.

Needs affect all aspects of your life.

At this point, Les has indicated that in relation to work, he has recorded the highest possible rating.

The language is positive. Les records he is "better than this," and his potential has yet to be realised.

By examining and evaluating the other recordings under desire, ability, and reason, you can identify that it is the work itself, not just the job, that is in review.

As you would expect, Les's ability to enjoy his leisure time is compromised by the pervasive negative images he is experiencing. Escalation of the urgency for change can manifest in less-than-desirable actions.

One of the goals of using DARNitCAT is that this method of evaluation promotes the best actions possible for you over irrational short-term behaviours.

The final summary of needs suggests that Les's real desire is to be confident in himself and rewarded for his efforts. Note that these two needs do not necessarily promote or endorse leaving his position and finding a new job.

As you reach this stage of evaluation, you can identify that there is a need to change the situation, not necessarily the total environment. The desire for a new job does not identify strongly. After review, it is clearly a situational issue, as the desire is strongly, extrinsically motivating.

Under ability, you can see that Les is quite negative about his prospects and quite rightly so; therefore, his perception of ability is low.

What comes through after looking at the reasons and needs Les has recorded is that they merely further strengthen the idea that changing his job is not a real intrinsic motivation. Changing elements of his current position may provide a more meaningful and achievable desire.

After your first evaluation of the four parts of DARN, you can see that what is lacking is ability. The first job is to focus on how to increase ability where ability is perceived to be low.

Reason and need endorse that there needs to be a change; however, these two components are negatively and extrinsically reinforced. They are not totally about Les; they are about others in his family and work environments.

You get a hint of what Les needs, but it does not signal there are prospects for a new job, at least not near where he lives (and with little certainty of success elsewhere, for that matter). He would be leaving the comfort of a negatively reinforcing position for the unknown in a different work and social environment.

Reviewing this under generic principles, it would be reasonable to suggest that Les's fear level would increase, expectations are unknown, what is necessary is hypothetical at best, and his habits definitely require change.

Les is likely to remain high in the domain under importance as far as change goes but not necessarily to the radical extent of a new job, as his initial desire stated.

His confidence recording would most likely be very low. This factor is supported because of his low level of ability, confirming his doubts as to whether the desire of obtaining a new job is realistic without significantly changing other variables, such as the area he is looking in.

At this point, the idea of seeking a new job seems unlikely. The positive issues he has described suggest that reviewing the initial desire may warrant looking at another approach and perhaps a modification of his desire.

Instead of a new job (that may or may not provide what Les desires), it may be worthwhile analysing his ability to change the conditions of his present position.

He could meet with his employer and outline his motivation to improve himself; this show that he's willing to accept new challenges, which is mutually favourable for both Les and his employer.

If there is room within his current position to turn it into one that is more favourable and that meets his expectations, this could be the focus of his new desire.

Broken down into several meaningful components, his real desire suggests it is a combination of recognition and reward for his effort and a need for more challenge in his work.

Never be afraid to change. You may lose something good, but you may gain something better.

—Anon.

6

Commitment, Action, and Taking Steps

If you've been reading this book as the first option mentioned in the introduction, this is where I'll leave you (for now, anyway; you can always come back and work with it in depth later, if you wish). However, hopefully you've decided to make a commitment to action and take steps towards some behavioural changes to achieve your desires.

By now, you should have a grasp of how your mental processes work in establishing goals and desires and then actually turning them into reality.

You have looked at your onion and seen how the impact of everyday issues, stresses, and commitments can become so overbearing that the concept of engaging in something unknown seems daunting, even though you know it may be beneficial to you.

If you separate the layers of your onion and review them as distinct issues, rather than one big one, you can reduce the intensity of tasks and effort required to help you deal with them.

Knowing who you are and what your motivators look like gives you an overview of how to recognise your shortcomings and celebrate your strengths.

It is imperative to recognise how fear affects you and how to confront it in any given situation, particularly when implementing change or venturing into an unknown realm.

The first step towards challenging current behaviour is to understand how expectations from your habits restrict you from moving towards your goals and prevents you from turning the perception of your desires into reality.

Being able to visualise the desire is the first step towards positive action.

You always have two choices: your commitment versus your fear.
—Sammy Davis Jr.

Commitment

I've covered all of the academic reviews of your motivation, what drives you, why you may succeed or fail, why you accept your current position, and how various conscious and subconscious drivers influence your life.

Hopefully, you will have started to consider what your dreams, aspirations, and desires look like.

Remember that your desires can be as extravagant as you like, limited only by your imagination.

The previous chapters demonstrated how you can identify your ability to turn imaginary concepts into reality. Evaluating reasons and needs reinforces the desires and helps you search for ways to increase your ability.

However, all of this is hypothetical until you put action into place. The likelihood of success of your actions is firmly enhanced by your commitment.

Commitment by itself is merely a pledge that you intend to do something after evaluating the benefits and investigating why you should not engage in a behaviour. However, it does not give details such as level of involvement, time allocation, promised results, or any other details. As an example, many politicians are committed to bringing about world peace but have failed to do it. In other words, there is no consequence, negative or positive, if your commitment does not amount to anything.

The first thing I do as a mentor is to listen. Not just to what my clients say but, more importantly, how they say it. Commitment language identifies the strength of the commitment.

Listen to what you're saying.

Here are several ways of looking at what your commitment looks like in the different ways you express it:

"I'm definitely doing this; I know I have the ability because of …. It will help me because it will … and if I don't, … will continue."

Strong commitment language is indicated with words such as "definitely," and phrases such as "I know" and "it will" further indicate this has been thought through. Motivation appears to be high.

Alternatively, alarm bells may ring if you hear this:

"I'd really like to do this, but …. I think it will …, and if it does, then I might …"

Commitment language is weak, at best. "I'd really like to" is tempered by a "but" condition. Conditions are always indicated by the word *but*. "I think" is a warning that there are reservations about doing something. Rather, it indicates that the concept hasn't been thought through, and there is not a clear visualisation of what the desire looks like.

Let's look at a simple situation with someone we'll call Bob and see how his commitment can be measured.

Commitment; Action; Taking Steps

Task	Level of Commitment	Action Idea	Perceived Success	Steps to Implement Action	Effectiveness of Steps
Get fit	8	Go for a walk	9	Put track suit and shoes on	7

In the example given, we can see Bob's idea of getting fit is strong. The indication is, he would clearly like to be fitter.

He recorded his desire (get fit), his ability (no medical reason to preclude the intervention of running), the reason (it would give him more energy), and need (if he doesn't, he could be at risk of health issues).

The perceived success of the action actually increases the idea that if he performs the action, he will get fitter. His doctor advises it as suitable; speaking with friends who run endorses the activity. (These elements assist Bob's ability through encouragement.)

However, after donning the appropriate attire to complete the task, his motivation has waned a little.

Fear may be related to attempting something you haven't done before, and if you've attempted it before and failed, this can have a profound negative effect. You may have failed before because you didn't put the right amount of effort in, or perhaps you didn't persevere for the required time to make a difference, or the intrinsic motivation to do it wasn't high enough.

Your commitment and action suggest your willingness to move, to make a change to target your goals. However, that doesn't necessarily mean anything, unless you actually take steps towards doing something.

Action

Action is the process of doing something; an action may simply be reading a book or watching a video that's linked to the goal driving the interest and the commitment level thus far. Action indicates there is a greater possibility of engagement than not, and if no engagement is instigated, this may indicate that either the goal is not intrinsically motivating enough or there is a fear of loss or some other negative consequence stemming from the perceived engagement.

There may be many forms of action prior to taking any steps. This can be considered as the evaluation stage. Evaluating the effort required, the current level of ability, and the commitment level should lead to taking steps to complete the goal.

You can action a commitment in your head; however, when you do, you are only simulating the action by visualising it. That is a normal process; you can see yourself completing the action without committing to physically doing anything.

If you do not turn that visualisation into taking steps, then perhaps your commitment level is not strong enough. If that's the case, it may be for one of these reasons:

- Your commitment isn't strong enough.
- You are unable to see how the action will move you towards your goal.
- There are stronger motivators pressing on you at this time.
- The motivation for the end goal is not strong enough in an intrinsic sense.

What now?

Well, you haven't failed.

- Go back and look at the end goal.
- Is it too ambitious at this stage?
- Are you unable to start taking steps because of something else taking your attention?
- Check your onion.
- Check your timetables; are you trying to take steps at the wrong time?

It's now time to start visualising your desire, identifying your motivation, and determining your ability to achieve satisfaction.

Taking Steps

Establishing a level of commitment and taking steps to achieve goals can take some time; however, procrastination is the enemy of success, and you should be prepared to do some tangible work as soon as possible. Taking time to practice on a simple goal and following the processes identified in previous chapters will ensure a greater chance of success when you move onto bigger and better things.

Your level of commitment and subsequent actions and taking the necessary steps are directly proportional to the level of intrinsic motivation you have for your desire. Constantly referring to the desire as you complete intermediate goals will keep you on track. There will undoubtedly be some unpleasant and difficult tasks that you will be required to complete. Remember to have rewards planned for you when you get through the tough times and keep your focus on the desire.

Remember again that motivation is a state, not a trait; keep indicators around you of what success looks like as you imagine it. Keep in mind the end result while completing the lesser (and perhaps sometimes more unpleasant) goals.

If your initial goal, for example, is to lose weight, remember that weight loss in itself should not be the end desire; what the weight loss will do for you and why you need it should be the focus of the desire. Losing weight is merely a goal towards it.

If making money is the desire, change that to what the money will do for you and why you need it. Therefore, making money is a goal towards what you desire to do with that money.

Stages of Change

It is important to recognise that there is likely to be some form of failure along the way to making a desire a reality. Changing behaviour is not always a smooth ride; in fact, there are likely to be a number of significant bumps along the way.

In 1983, James Prochaska and Carlo DiClemente produced their findings on the stages of change.

They proposed that in any change in behaviour, there is a sequence of mental assessments that you will investigate and satisfy during the process. You will start with a pre-contemplative stage. During this phase, you will identify your desire and consider the benefits for you as well as what you perceive the likely investment is required.

There is no commitment to making any change or engaging in any different behaviour at this stage.

When the intrinsic motivation appears to be high, you will move forward to a contemplative phase. Here, you will recognise the need to do something. You will weigh up the plus and minus components of what is required to turn a desire into a reality.

Next, you will enter a phase where you prepare to engage in the behaviours and changes you need to make. You will look at things such as the resources you have, finances, time, and ability.

Once you're satisfied you have the necessary tools to begin, you will enter the action phase. Here, you may start with some trepidation; that is a normal reaction. Ensure you set achievable time frames as you set and complete essential goals. Remember to reward yourself for significant effort.

As you complete tasks, ensure that you've allocated time in your schedule to maintain the goals you've already achieved as you move on to more complex goals. This is your maintenance phase. It's also a time to reflect on whether you are still on track towards achieving your desires.

There is provision in the stages of change to recognise a relapse phase. Lack of attention to detail, not maintaining behavioural commitment, or setting goals too big can result in a relapse. This means your motivation has waned, or a more desirable motivator has steered you away from your goal. Remember? Motivation is a state, not a trait.

Although there is at some point a termination phase, which suggests that you have maintained the necessary behavioural change to achieve your ultimate desire, it is still important to review goals and desires to ensure you are still living the way you want and receiving the same expectation from your actions.

A failure is not always a mistake; it may simply be the best one can do under the circumstances. The real mistake is to stop trying.
—B. F. Skinner

The blank data sheets that follow will assist you in recording what you desire; your ability to achieve it; your reason for the desire; and why you need it.

If you would like assistance to get you through any areas identified in the chapters of this book, see the programmes available on our website, Micksmithmentor.com.

The following pages provide charts for you to start logging in the various parameters that are personal to you.

- identify your onion
- learn about where your particular motivation comes from
- study what it is you want and why
- evaluate what your fears, expectations, necessities, and habits look like.
- promote your desires
- identify your abilities
- consider your reasons
- listen to your needs

- check your commitment
- put your plan into action
- take steps every day

The best achievement in life is to do something you thought you couldn't.

—Anon.

Fear

Object of Fear	Frequency	Family	Work	Leisure	Intensity Overall Rating

Necessities

Object of Fear	Frequency	Family	Work	Leisure	Intensity Overall Rating

Expectation

Object of Fear	Frequency	Family	Work	Leisure	Intensity Overall Rating

Habit

Object of Fear	Frequency	Family	Work	Leisure	Intensity Overall Rating

Desire

Goal	Perceived Strength of Desire	Family	Work	Leisure	Overall Level of Desire

Ability

Goal	Perceived Level of Ability	Family	Work	Leisure	Overall Level of Ability

Reason

Goal	Perceived Strength of Reason	Family	Work	Leisure	Overall Strength of Reason

Need

Goal	Perceived Strength of Need	Family	Work	Leisure	Overall Strength of Need

Commitment; Action; Taking Steps

Task	Level of Commitment	Action Idea	Perceived Success of Action	Steps Taken to Implement Action	Effectiveness of Steps Taken

Importance

Situation	Overall	Work	Family	Leisure	After Consideration

Confidence

Situation	Overall	Work	Family	Leisure	After Consideration

About the Author

Mick Smith is a Canadian-born resident of New Zealand, where he lives on a small farm with his wife, Kath, and their menagerie of horses and other animals. He is the father of two children (who both reside overseas) and the doting grandfather of one.

He is a keen collector and restorer of American cars from the thirties to the sixties.

His vocational history began by attending teachers' college, where he studied educational psychology. A sabbatical from teaching led to completing a certificate in mechanical engineering; he utilised these skills to design and build orthopaedic equipment for rehabilitating patients with spinal cord injuries.

A passion for assisting others led to a career as a professional firefighter; unfortunately, he sustained critical injuries. After being disappointed with the mental and physical rehabilitation he was subjected to, Mick furthered his studies in psychology, attaining special qualifications in cognitive behavioural therapy and clinical psychology while working on his own rehabilitation.

Mick has a bachelor's in psychology, a postgraduate diploma in cognitive behavioural therapy, and a master's in philosophy in rehabilitation from Massey University in New Zealand, where he researched rehabilitation modalities for spinal cord injury patients. His PhD study concentrated on the prevention of secondary stroke.

He is a former board member of the New Zealand Rehabilitation Association and is a member of International Network of Motivational Interviewing Trainers (MINT).

Thirty years post-accident, Mick has been an avid rodeo rider, sports coach, and mentor to numerous athletes, including Olympic and Commonwealth games participants and the New Zealand All Blacks.

For a number of years, Mick was the senior rehabilitation advisor to the New Zealand government while lecturing on innovations in rehabilitation and motivational interviewing, both in New Zealand and overseas.

Today, Mick runs a private clinic for industry and individual clients and is working on his website and Internet blog.

Printed in the United States
By Bookmasters